WHALES, DOLPHINS, AND PORPOISES IN THE ZOO

BY ROLAND SMITH

Photographs by WILLIAM MUÑOZ

THE NEW ZOO
THE MILLBROOK PRESS
BROOKFIELD, CT.

All photographs copyright © 1994 by William Muñoz,
except pages 25 (top), 27, 58 (top) courtesy Mel
Woods, and page 58 (bottom) © Roland Smith.

Library of Congress Cataloging-in-Publication Data
Smith, Roland, 1951–
Whales, dolphins, and porpoises in the zoo / by Roland Smith;
photographs by William Muñoz.
p.   cm.—(The New zoo)
Includes bibliographical references (p.   ) and index.
Summary: Describes various marine mammals
and their care in oceanariums,
discussing capture and training methods.
ISBN 1-56294-318-9 (lib. bdg.)
1. Cetacea—Juvenile literature.   2. Zoo animals—Juvenile
literature. [1. Whales.   2. Dolphins.   3. Porpoises.   4. Zoo
animals.]   I. Muñoz, William, ill.   II. Title.   III. Series: Smith,
Roland, 1951–   New zoo.
SF408.6.C47S58   1994
636'.95—dc20   93-35425   CIP   AC

Published by the Millbrook Press
2 Old New Milford Road
Brookfield, Connecticut 06804

Contents

The author and photographer
wish to thank the following
organizations and individuals
for their help with this book:

Lowry Park Zoo
Point Defiance Zoo & Aquarium
Sea World
Marie K. Smith
Bethany Kreilcamp
and John Houck

Introduction

In the past, before we began to understand the harmful effects we were having on the earth and its wildlife, a zoo's main function was to entertain and amuse its human visitors. Today, many of the animals kept in zoos are not there just for our entertainment. They are also there because it is no longer safe for them in the wild, and they are in danger of becoming extinct.

We could compare the new zoos to Noah's Ark—"lifeboats" with human keepers for rescuing animals in danger of extinction. During the "voyage," the keepers do everything they can to make sure that the animals survive and, if possible, reproduce in their artificial environment.

While the keepers are caring for the animals, biologists are looking for wild habitat to which some of the animals might be returned. In the biblical story of Noah's Ark, after the flood there were very few people on earth and vast wilderness areas. Today, there are many people and very few wilderness areas.

Throughout history there have been stories about people's relationships with whales, dolphins, and porpoises. These wonderful marine mammals become tame very quickly. Gray whales and killer whales have been known to swim right up to boats and actually let people scratch their backs.

Not long ago, off the coast of New Zealand, there was a wild dolphin who regularly let children ride on its back and took part in games of catch with a beach ball. This friendly behavior and natural curiosity is common in almost all whales, dolphins, and porpoises.

Unfortunately, this same curiosity and fearlessness have led to the near extinction of many whales because they were not able to distinguish between friendly people and people like whalers, who meant them harm.

Some people believe that whales, dolphins, and porpoises are the most intelligent creatures in the animal kingdom. Not only do they have a sophisticated way of communicating, they are also known to help each other when injured. Dolphins have been seen supporting an unconscious companion so that it can breathe on the surface of the water. This behavior has also been observed in humpback whales and gray whales. Sperm whales will travel great distances when they hear the distress call of another whale.

This book is about whales, dolphins, and porpoises in captivity—where they come from, what they are like, and how they are cared for.

Zoos and oceanariums are places where visitors personally experience these ocean creatures. Without this experience, few of us would have the opportunity to see whales, dolphins, and porpoises. It is hoped that after people have seen these magnificent creatures in the zoo, they will want to help to protect them in the wild. In many ways their future depends on us.

A killer whale opens wide for a meal.

Whales, Dolphins, and Porpoises

Before we look at how whales, dolphins, and porpoises are cared for in zoos and oceanariums, we must first understand a few things about how they function in their watery natural environment.

Like us, whales, dolphins, and porpoises are mammals — that is, they are warm-blooded and suckle their young. Like other mammals, they have lungs and breathe air. This means they must come to the surface of the water to breathe. Fish, on the other hand, have gills, which they use to get oxygen from the water.

Scientifically, whales, dolphins, and porpoises are classified as *cetaceans* (pronounced seh-TAY-shuns). That word is from the Latin *cetus*, meaning "a large sea creature."

Cetaceans are divided into two primary categories: toothed whales and baleen whales (pronounced bay-LEAN). Because dolphins and porpoises have teeth, they are classified with the toothed whales.

The most common toothed whales kept in captivity are the common dolphin, bottle-nosed dolphin, porpoise, beluga whale, pilot whale, Pacific killer whale, and false killer whale.

The largest toothed whale, the sperm whale, has never been kept in captivity because of its size. Sperm whales reach lengths of more than 60 feet (18 meters) and can weigh nearly 100,000 pounds (45,360 kilograms)! Two of the smallest toothed whales kept in captivity are the common dolphin and the harbor porpoise.

Toothed whales feed primarily on fish and can be found in coastal waters where fish are abundant. In fact, fishermen look for these whales, knowing that they will lead them to schools of fish.

Baleen whales include the pygmy right whale, California gray whale, blue whale, finback whale, bowhead whale, sei whale, Atlantic right whale, minke whale, and humpback whale.

Instead of teeth, baleen whales have rows of fibrous material (called baleen) that they use to filter or trap food before it goes into their gigantic three-chambered stomachs. They feed primarily on krill, which are different kinds of very tiny marine organisms. To eat, baleen whales swim through clouds of krill with their mouths open. The whales force the water out between the broomlike baleen plates, trapping tens of thousands of krill, which they then swallow. No one knows exactly how much krill a baleen whale eats a day, but it is certainly hundreds to thousands of pounds. One reason that baleen whales are not kept in captivity is that it is nearly impossible to provide enough krill for them to survive.

The largest baleen whale is the blue whale, which can

reach a length of 110 feet (33 meters) and weigh nearly a half a million pounds (226,800 kilograms)! The blue whale is actually the largest animal that has ever existed—bigger than the largest dinosaur that ever lived. The smallest baleen whale is the pygmy right whale, which reaches a maximum length of 21 feet (6 meters) and can weigh up to 8,000 pounds (3,600 kilograms).

Baby cetaceans · The *gestation period* (time of pregnancy) is quite long in cetaceans—from 9.5 to 17 months, depending on the species. They have a single offspring, which is one fourth to one third the length of the mother. A baby cetacean can swim immediately after it is born.

Whales, dolphins, and porpoises are born tailfirst. This is just the opposite of land mammals, which deliver their youngsters headfirst. As soon as the baby is born, its mother gently pushes it to the surface where it opens its blowhole and takes its first breath of air. Soon after this, the mother turns her body to the side and encourages the baby to nurse.

Young cetaceans grow very fast due to the rich milk their mothers provide. The milk has a very high fat content (40 percent), and it contains twice the protein of land-mammal milk.

Mothers are very protective toward their youngsters during the first several months of their lives. They don't allow the babies to stray too far away and will prevent them from approaching new objects in the pool.

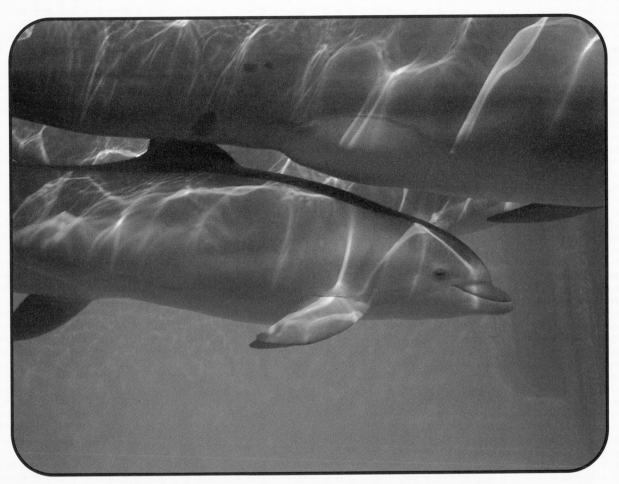

A bottle-nosed dolphin calf swims close to its mother.
For the first few months of life, baby cetaceans remain under
the constant care and protection of their mothers.

As with all mother-youngster relationships, this protectiveness eventually decreases. At 6 months, the young cetaceans begin to eat small amounts of solid food. By the time they are 18 months, they are weaned off milk and left pretty much on their own to find food within the group.

Whale characteristics · Whales, dolphins, and porpoises have many unique physical and behavioral characteristics that help them survive in the ocean.

For instance, a cetacean's nostrils are on the top its head. This allows it to breathe without exposing much of its body above the surface of the water. This opening on the head is called the blowhole. Toothed whales have one blowhole, and baleen whales have two. Before taking a breath, whales and dolphins exhale with great force through the blowhole, pushing most of the air out of their lungs. By emptying their lungs in this way they are able to take more air in and stay underwater longer. On cold days, when they exhale, the warm air from the lungs hits the cool air and becomes mist.

Each type of whale has a unique blow, or spout, and experts can distinguish among species by observing the characteristics of the blow. The right whale's blow is 9 to 12 feet (3 to 4 meters) high. The sperm whale has a blow nearly 22 feet (7 meters) high.

Whales, dolphins, and porpoises are able to stay warm in very cold water. Two *adaptations* help to keep them warm: a thick blubber layer that insulates them, and a high *metabolism*

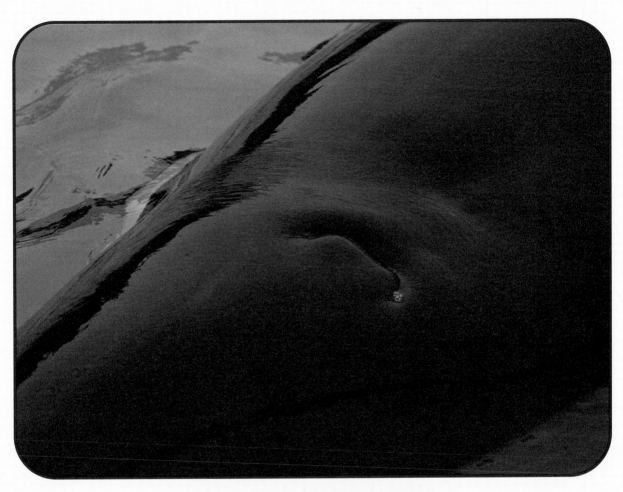

The blowhole of a killer whale.
Because it is toothed, this whale has only
one blowhole. Baleen whales have two.

A veterinarian checks a killer whale's
tail fluke. Unlike fish, which move their
tails from side to side, cetaceans move
their tails up and down.

that must be constantly fueled by large amounts of food. Besides heat, this high metabolism also produces energy.

Instead of arms and legs, whales have flippers and tail flukes. Unlike fish, which have vertical tails that move from side to side, whales and dolphins have horizontal tails, which they move up and down to propel them forward.

Their bodies are shaped aerodynamically, like bullets, allowing them to move rapidly through the water. In general, large whales rarely exceed 6 miles an hour (5 knots), but the smaller dolphins and porpoises can move at speeds of over 28 miles an hour (25 knots).

The senses · Most cetaceans have good eyesight above and below the water. But perhaps the most unique adaptation that toothed whales have is their ability to use *sonar*, or echolocation, to orient themselves and to find food. With the ability to echolocate, cetaceans are less dependent on their eyesight than other mammals.

Cetaceans are constantly emitting high-pitched sound waves above and below water. When these waves hit a solid object, the sound bounces back toward the animal. With its incredible sensing ability, a cetacean can tell exactly what the object is.

Captive cetaceans have been trained to wear blindfolds (harmless soft rubber suction cups placed comfortably over the eyes). With blindfolds on they are able to tell the difference between a piece of dead fish and an object exactly the same size. In one experiment like this, a blindfolded dolphin was able to find and pick up half a vitamin tablet on the bottom of the pool. Needless to say, cetaceans have very good hearing.

Can whales, dolphins, and porpoises talk? ·
Cetaceans are able to produce a wide variety of sounds, and they can certainly communicate with each other and with their trainers, but most experts do not consider this the ability to talk in the traditional sense.

All animals are able to communicate with each other on some level. Sometimes this communication is behavioral—a body posture or a facial expression. Sometimes communication is vocal—like a dog growling to keep you away, or whining to let you know that it wants something. But this is not talking. As far as we know, human beings are the only animals on earth that are able to use complex verbal language to talk to each other.

But, as we will see in Chapter Four, cetaceans *are* able to understand some human words and actions—much as dogs can understand when we tell them to "sit," "stay," or "come." They learn these words by associating the repeated word with a *behavior*.

Now that we know something about cetacean characteristics, we'll take a close look at how whales, dolphins, and porpoises are captured, handled, and transported.

Bottle-nosed dolphins arc from the water in formation.

Capture, Transport, and Handling

Although some cetaceans are born in captivity, many of the animals in zoos and oceanariums are taken from the wild.

Capturing wild animals is a controversial issue. Many animal rights activists say that cetaceans kept in captivity (even under the best circumstances) do not do as well as they would if left in the wild.

Zoos and oceanariums, on the other hand, say that by taking a few of these animals into captivity much has been learned about their behavior, reproductive habits, and care. With this knowledge, biologists have been able to help cetaceans in the wild.

Each side of this issue has a valid point of view. The animal rights activists help to make sure that zoos take the best possible care of cetaceans in captivity. By displaying cetaceans, zoos help millions of people reach a new understanding of cetaceans in the wild. In fact, the popularity of whales, dolphins, and porpoises is due in large part to people's ability to see them up close in their captive environment.

Permits · Before an oceanarium or zoo in the United States takes a cetacean from the wild, it must first obtain a collection permit from the federal government. All marine mammals in the United States fall under the jurisdiction of a law called the Marine Mammal Protection Act.

Permission to take a cetacean from the wild takes several months and is not easy to get. Before the government issues a collection permit, it carefully inspects the captive facility where the cetacean is going, making certain that the oceanarium or zoo meets all of the standards set forth by the law:

- Its pools must be big enough and have superb water quality.
- Its staff must be very experienced in caring for cetaceans.
- The facility must prove that it has enough money to do the expensive job of feeding and caring for cetaceans.

Once the captive facility has been approved, the government considers whether the collection request is in the best interest of the animals being taken from the wild.

The permit is very specific and outlines exactly what can and cannot be done by the crew capturing the cetaceans. Included in the permit are:

- The species being captured
- The exact dates the capture is going to take place
- The reasons for taking the animals from the wild (public display, education, scientific research, etc.)
- The location of the capture

- The exact number, the sex, and the approximate age of the cetaceans to be captured
- The method of capture
- How the animals are going to be transported after the capture

After the details of the permit are worked out, the request is sent to marine mammal experts for review. After this, the permit application is made public. In this way, members of the public and environmental groups can comment on it. Every letter and comment for or against the capture is considered and responded to. The government wants to make certain that the capture will ultimately benefit the species and in no way harm it.

To ensure the safety of the animals, a qualified marine mammal veterinarian must be on hand during the capture, and the crew must have extensive experience in the successful capture of cetaceans in the wild. Zoos and oceanariums do not take the capture of wild cetaceans lightly. They are deeply concerned about the welfare of the animals.

As you can see, getting a collection permit to capture a cetacean is not easy. This is a good thing, because it protects whales, dolphins, and porpoises from people who are not qualified to care for them.

The capture · Whales, dolphins, and porpoises are relatively easy to catch. Generally the capture crew has a pretty good idea of the whereabouts and behavior of the group it wants to capture.

One method of capture is to use a large net to encircle the group, in much the same way that fishermen net fish. Once the group of cetaceans is encircled, the net is drawn up around the cetaceans, and divers enter the water to select and hand-restrain the animals they want to keep.

Another method is to use small boats to herd the group or individual animals into shallow water. Once the animals are in the shallows, two or three divers jump out of the boats and hold the animals until they can be put in the boats.

Many dolphins and porpoises seem to enjoy swimming next to, or in front of, speeding boats. Capture crews are sometimes able to take advantage of this behavior by throwing a net over an animal swimming next to a boat.

The reason divers go into the water with the cetaceans is to make sure the animals don't get tangled in the nets and injure themselves. Going in with animals like this can be risky to the diver because he or she could be injured by a swat from the cetacean's powerful tail. Although toothed whales are *carnivores*, feeding primarily on the flesh of other animals, they rarely try to bite people.

Remarkably, most cetaceans calm down very quickly and stop struggling once they are in the net. The animals that the crew doesn't want are set free. The remaining animals are gently guided into specially designed slings or stretchers and carefully lifted onto the boat.

*Divers have placed a beluga whale in a sling
so that it can be transported into captivity.
Slings are heavily padded to prevent the
animal being cut or bruised while being moved.
Holes also allow flippers to hang freely.*

The slings are heavily padded with foam rubber to prevent abrasions and pressure sores. Cetaceans are not used to being out of water, and their bodies are designed for *buoyancy*. If they are put on a hard surface for any length of time, pressure sores develop, which can be a severe problem. In addition to the padding, the slings are made with cutouts so the cetaceans' flippers will be able to move freely without getting pinched.

Stranders · A few of the cetaceans kept by zoos and oceanariums are there because they were found stranded on the beach or shore. No one knows for sure why whales, dolphins, and porpoises strand.

Although mass strandings occur, generally strandings involve a single animal or a mother and her young calf. The stranded animal is often found to be injured in some way. Unfortunately, by the time the zoo or oceanarium is contacted about the stranding, it may be too late to save the animal. Most *stranders* do not survive. The few stranders that do live are rarely released after they recover because rehabilitation often takes a long time and release back into the wild is seldom successful.

Transport · After the animals have been captured they are usually rushed to shore and placed in a temporary holding pool near the site of the capture. When the cetaceans have calmed down and gotten used to their new pool, the veterinarian does a physical examination to make sure the animals are healthy and have not been injured during the capture. The next step is to transport the cetaceans to the zoo or oceanarium.

If the animals are to be transported long distances, aircraft are used. This can be very expensive because very few commercial airlines provide this service. Depending on the number and size of the animals, zoos often must rent an airplane to move the animals.

Transporting cetaceans is often the most hazardous part of collecting them. They are simply not designed to be out of water for long. And shipping them in water is usually out of the question. The large volume of water they require is simply too heavy for most airplanes. So, cetaceans are generally shipped in slings or stretchers.

Whales, dolphins, and porpoises have very delicate and complex heating and cooling systems. When a cetacean is out of the water, one of the most dangerous problems is that it might overheat. To help eliminate this, attendants make sure that the cetacean is constantly wetted down. They use sprayers and often place wet towels on the animal's body to make sure that it stays moist and cool. During transport the cetacean's temperature is constantly monitored. If the temperature is rising, ice water is poured on the flippers and tail fluke to cool the cetacean down. In severe cases of overheating, the animal might be packed with ice all around it.

Another problem for the cetacean out of water is that its skin begins to dry out. To prevent this, the animal is smeared with zinc oxide cream and lanolin, which help to keep its skin moist and also to lessen chafing and abrasions while the animal is in the stretcher.

When cetaceans must travel long distances to zoos and oceanariums, they sometimes go by airplane. But the animals' size, weight, and water requirements make this method of transportation expensive and inconvenient.

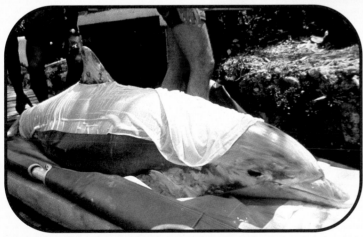

This bottle-nosed dolphin in transit has been smeared with special cream and covered with wet cloths so that its skin remains moist and its temperature stable.

If a serious problem arises with an animal during transport, there is little anyone can do about it because of the limited working space on an airplane. Needless to say, the quicker the transport, the better it is for the animal.

When the airplane touches down at the final destination, trucks, cranes, and an experienced ground crew are waiting to move the cetaceans to the zoo or oceanarium.

At the oceanarium the animal (still in its stretcher) is gently placed into a holding pool. Generally the water level in the pool is lowered in case the animal has trouble swimming after the long transport. In addition to this, divers are in the water to help keep it buoyant until it adjusts.

A newly arrived animal is watched 24 hours a day until the oceanarium staff is certain that it is swimming vigorously and feeding properly.

In the next chapter we will take a close look at how cetaceans are cared for in their new home.

Beluga whales are fed.

Caring for Whales, Dolphins, and Porpoises

In order for cetaceans to do well in captivity, everything in their aquatic environment must be perfect, including the design and size of the pool, the water quality, their food, and the care they receive from their keepers.

Exhibit design · Cetaceans are kept in large saltwater pools. The size of the pool depends on the size and number of cetaceans being held. Some pools look like swimming pools. Others look naturalistic — that is, they're designed to look like the cetaceans' natural ocean environment.

In addition to the main viewing pool, there are adjacent smaller holding pools (usually off-exhibit) where the cetaceans are put while the main pool is cleaned. These holding pools are also used for sick or injured animals and for new arrivals.

Many pools have underwater viewing windows so that visitors can see the beauty and grace of cetaceans swimming.

There is usually a training and feeding platform on the surface of the pool where keepers and trainers can feed and interact with the animals. Across from the platform is a view-

A training platform is an important part of any cetacean's zoo or oceanarium home. This killer whale has learned to come out of the water onto a training platform so that it can be examined.

ing area so the public can watch the animal shows or demonstrations.

Unlike keepers of land mammals, keepers of cetaceans don't have to worry about their animals escaping from the exhibit. Water represents security to cetaceans, and they are not about to leave it. Therefore, the barriers you see around pools are designed to keep people out, not to keep the animals in.

Aside from keeping people out of the pools, the barriers are also designed to prevent people from dropping things in the water, like sunglasses, purses, cameras, etc. Cetaceans are very curious, and if someone accidentally drops something in the pool an animal is bound to pick it up and start playing with it. This can be very dangerous for the animal because it might accidentally (or intentionally) swallow the object. Swallowing a foreign object is sometimes called hardware disease. The object can block the intestines and do other damage that could lead to the animal's death.

This can be such a serious problem that on crowded days oceanariums will have someone constantly watching the visitors around the pool. If a visitor drops something in the pool, the keepers are notified immediately so they can attempt to get it away from the cetacean before it swallows the object. Sometimes this means going into the water to get the object. If the animal is holding the object, keepers will try to exchange it for a piece of food or something else that the animal wants. If the animal does swallow the object, the veterinarian must be called in to treat it.

Water • Water quality is perhaps the most important key to keeping cetaceans healthy in captivity. The water in which they live must have the right amount of salinity (salt) and the correct temperature and be free of harmful chemicals and pollutants.

Many oceanariums are built near the sea so they can take advantage of the unlimited supply of natural salt water. Other oceanariums are located inland and must make salt water for their cetaceans.

Whether the salt water is natural or artificial, it must pass through a complex filtration system before it goes into the pool. Filtering the water removes harmful contaminants like dead food, waste, and bacteria. Ideally, oceanariums like to see the water in the pool undergo a complete change every two or three hours.

How often a pool is emptied for a thorough cleaning depends on the efficiency of the filtration system. The water quality is tested several times each day. If the contaminant level is too high, the cetaceans are put in the holding pool while the main pool is drained and cleaned.

During the summer, pools are cleaned more often because the long days of sunlight cause *algae* to grow. These algae blooms are not necessarily harmful to cetaceans, but they can make it difficult to see the animals.

Feeding cetaceans • Cetaceans have to be fed a great amount of food to fuel their high metabolism. A dolphin is fed

15 pounds (7 kilograms) of food a day. An adult killer whale will put away a whopping 125 pounds (57 kilograms) of food a day! Obviously, feeding cetaceans can be very expensive.

Among the fish fed to whales, dolphins, and porpoises are mackerel, smelt, whitefish, and herring. Generally, to save on costs, zoos and oceanariums buy their fish in huge quantities. The fish is stored in large walk-in freezers, and just enough food is thawed out to feed the animals that day.

While some newly arrived cetaceans will eat dead fish immediately, others will refuse to eat for several days after they arrive in captivity. Getting new cetaceans to eat is extremely important. Although many other animals can go for a period of time without food and not starve, cetaceans must eat because they receive all of their fresh water from fish. If they refuse to eat they can become dehydrated and die. Just like us, cetaceans cannot drink salt water.

Keepers patiently encourage reluctant feeders to eat. A few live fish might be put in the tank along with the usual meal of dead fish. Eventually the cetacean's hunger overtakes its reluctance and it accepts the new type of food.

The amount of fish fed each day is carefully weighed out each morning. How much fish each animal gets every day is carefully monitored. The amount fed depends on the species and its physical condition. If an animal is too heavy, the amount of food is cut back. Being overweight can cause problems for cetaceans, just as it can for humans.

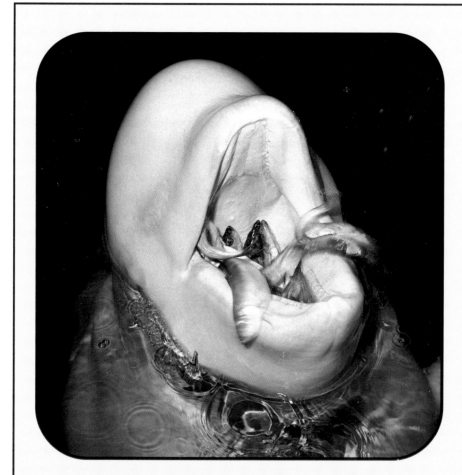

A beluga whale shows off a mouthful of mackerel. Because of their size, captive cetaceans must be fed many pounds of fish daily.

Generally, each cetacean has its own personal feed bucket with its name written on it (or several buckets in the case of a large cetacean like a killer whale). This helps the keeper keep track of how much food each animal has eaten that day.

To supplement the cetacean's diet, vitamins are slipped into the first few fish fed during the day. This is called pilling. Cetaceans usually don't even know they are being pilled because, unlike many other animals, they swallow their food whole without chewing it.

Because cetaceans need such large quantities of food, they are fed several times a day. Often these feeds take place as part of training sessions or shows, which we will discuss in greater detail in Chapter Four.

Cetacean medicine · Cetaceans can get many of the same diseases as humans: stomach ulcers, eye and ear infections, respiratory troubles, skin infections, heart disease, bacterial infections, arthritis, cancer, and tooth decay. Even a case of tonsillitis has been reported.

The first line of defense against these and other diseases is preventive medicine and early detection. Keepers pay very close attention to the cetaceans under their care. Among the things they look for are abnormal breathing, loss of appetite, changes in the consistency of feces or urine, or abnormal discharges from the eyes, blowhole, or mouth. Often a change in behavior can indicate a disease problem. The animal might become less active than normal; it might swim in a different pattern or refuse food. All these are reasons for concern. If the behavior continues, a veterinarian is called in to examine the cetacean.

Marine mammal medicine is a very specialized field, and there are very few veterinarians who practice it. In fact, marine mammal veterinarians are often flown all over the country to treat sick and injured cetaceans.

The first thing keepers do when they suspect that a cetacean is ill is to draw blood from it. By having the blood analyzed they can usually tell if the animal is suffering from infection and, if so, how bad the infection is.

Many cetaceans have been trained to lay their tail flukes on the training platform so routine blood samples can be drawn. This eliminates the need to take the animal out of the water to draw the blood. Such training not only saves the animal a lot of undue stress, but it also saves the keepers a lot of time and effort.

Some diseases can be treated by giving the cetacean oral *antibiotics*. And as we have learned, pilling a cetacean is relatively easy. If for some reason the animal is not eating well or refuses the medicated fish, antibiotic injections may have to be given.

Not all diseases or problems can be cured with antibiotic treatments. One such problem is hardware disease, in which the cetacean swallows an object that blocks the intestinal tract. If the object is not removed, the animal will die. To treat this problem, the cetacean is taken out of the water, laid on a thick foam-rubber mat to prevent abrasions and pressure sores, and *anesthetized*. To find out where the object is inside the animal, an instrument called a laparoscope is used.

Laparoscopes are used to look inside an animal's throat and stomach without having to do surgery. The scope is a long thin tube attached to an eyepiece for viewing. At the end of the tube is a lens and a light so the veterinarian can see what he or she is looking at. The tube is gently put down the animal's throat until it reaches the blockage. If the object is small, often it can be removed with an attachment to the laparoscope called a grabber. If the object is too big for the grabber and is not too far down the throat, a person with thin arms will try to get the object out by grabbing it by hand. If this doesn't work, surgery will have to be performed to remove the object.

To help prevent disease, cetaceans are given physical exams by the veterinarian at least once or twice a year. For exams, cetaceans are taken out of the water and placed on foam pads. Then blood is taken, the stomach is checked with a laparoscope, and, in the case of an adult female, an ultrasound exam might be made to see if she is pregnant. Ultrasound machines work in a similar way to sonar and echolocation. A sound wave is transmitted through the body and bounces off the developing baby in the womb. The resulting echo is translated into a picture on a screen that looks like a television. By

Veterinarians perform an ultrasound exam on a pregnant bottle-nose dolphin. They use a device that emits sound waves into the mother's body. Inset: A computer translates the sound waves into a video image of her baby's head.

analyzing this picture, the veterinarian can estimate when the baby cetacean is going to be born and how it is doing.

Veterinary care is greatly enhanced if the cetacean being treated is well trained. In the next chapter we will take a close look at how these animals are trained.

A killer whale leaps from the water to touch its target.

Training Whales, Dolphins, and Porpoises

*T*raining whales, dolphins, and porpoises reaches far beyond putting on shows for the public. Not only is training a valuable *husbandry* tool. It keeps the cetaceans active and alert in captivity. It also provides a way to exercise them in order to keep them healthy and fit. In addition to this, training helps to establish a working relationship between the animal and human. The interaction that takes place during training deepens our understanding of the animal. In a sense, the training process establishes a common language between the trainer and the animal.

We are delighted when we see a group of dolphins burst out of the water like rockets in perfect unison. We marvel at the trainer's ability to make a killer whale float on its back, or to have several beluga whales all "sing" at the same time. How does a trainer do this?

A horse is trained with a bridle and lead rope. A dog is trained with a collar and leash. But you cannot use this equipment on a cetacean. Fish is the primary tool used to train whales, dolphins, and porpoises, along with a training method known as operant conditioning. This word makes training sound very technical, but you are probably more familiar with this training theory than you think.

Reinforcement · Training is based on two types of *reinforcement*—positive and negative. An example of a positive reinforcement is giving your dog a piece of food after it sits on your command. An example of a negative reinforcement is jerking on your dog's collar to make it come with you. With cetaceans, trainers use only positive reinforcement (with one minor exception, which we will talk about later).

The whole theory of training is to reward behavior that is likely to be repeated. If your dog sits and you give it a treat, it is likely that it will sit again in order to get another treat. If a whale jumps out of the water and is rewarded for this behavior with a fish, it is likely that it will jump out of the water again in order to get another fish.

One of the most important aspects of training is timing your reinforcement correctly. If you tell your dog to sit and it is back on its feet by the time you give it the reward, the dog might think that you are telling it to stand.

How do trainers reward an animal that is 50 feet (15 meters) away? They create something called a conditioned reinforcer. In fact, creating a conditioned reinforcer is the first thing that trainers do when they begin to train a cetacean.

An example of a conditioned reinforcer is saying "good" to your dog when it does something you want it to do. Your dog associates the word *good* with something positive like food or a

**Using a whistle and hand signals, this trainer teaches
a white-sided dolphin to jump out of the water.**

pat on the head. You can say the word *good* to your dog much faster then you can give it a treat, and therefore it is often a more accurate reinforcer.

To create a conditioned reinforcer the trainer couples, or pairs, a sound with a food reward. The most common sound used as a conditioned reinforcer for cetaceans is a police whistle. The sound of the whistle becomes much like the word *good* that you use on your dog. A whistle is used because it sends out a clear consistent sound, and it frees up the trainer's hands for signaling and throwing fish.

A conditioned reinforcer is created by blowing the whistle and throwing the animal a fish over and over again, until the animal associates the sound with the reward. In this way, when the animal is 50 feet away and does the desired behavior, the trainer can reinforce this immediately by blowing the whistle. The cetacean then swims over to get its fish reward. With a conditioned reinforcer you have a way of communicating to the animal what you like about its behavior at exactly the right moment.

One powerful technique that trainers use to get solid behaviors from cetaceans is to *not* reward the animal every time it does a behavior right. This is called variable or random reinforcement. If a dolphin is given a reward every time it jumps, pretty soon it might become lazy and not put much effort into the jumps. In other words, it will try to get away with as little effort as possible to get its reward. If the trainer does not reward the first jump, the second jump will be stronger. If the second jump is not rewarded, the third jump may be stronger yet. To use this technique, trainers have to know their animal very well. One thing trainers don't want is to have the animal give up on the behavior because it thinks that it is not going to be rewarded for it.

How big a reward to use depends on the size of the animal. Generally, a reward consists of a small mouthful of food—just enough to keep the cetacean interested in the training session. As a general guideline, if there is one training session a day, the cetacean works well for about a quarter of its daily ration. When the training session is over, the rest of the cetacean's food is given to it for free. If there are three or four training sessions a day, trainers will divide the food into about eighty reinforcements and give twenty or thirty of them during each session.

Jackpot rewards are often given to a cetacean for doing a behavior particularly well—like a very high jump out of the water. Instead of getting one or two fish, the animal is given a huge handful in order to reinforce the high jump.

Regardless of how well or poorly a cetacean does during a training session or show, it is never starved or deprived of food—it always gets its full ration of fish.

Fish are not the only reward used to reinforce cetaceans. Other rewards might include scratching or rubbing their bodies or giving them a favorite toy to play with. Using different rewards keeps animals interested in the training session.

The only negative reinforcement used on cetaceans is a technique called a time-out. Time-outs are rarely used, but they can be very effective. If the animals are paying no attention during the training session, the trainer simply picks up the fish bucket, walks away, and stays out of sight for ten minutes or a half hour or more. Generally, when the trainer returns with the fish bucket the animals are more than willing to get on with the training session.

Stations, targets, and shaping · One of the first things that whales, dolphins, and porpoises are taught to do is to station. This is very much like telling a dog to stay in a certain place for a prolonged period of time. The cetacean is taught where to stay in the pool until the trainer calls the animal away from the station.

To help the animal learn where its station is, buoys are often used. When the cetacean touches its head on the buoy it is given a reward. The longer it stays on station, the more reinforcement it is given. Eventually the animal learns that during a training session or show it is to stay on station until the trainer calls it away from the station. The station is like a home base for the animal. It returns to its station for a reward after doing a behavior, and it stays on its station while the trainer is working with other animals in the pool. During a performance or training session, the trainer periodically throws a fish to the animals at their stations in order to reward them for staying there.

Four bottle-nosed dolphins assemble before a trainer at their station.

With a hand signal, the trainer has conditioned the dolphins to turn from the station and rise from water.

One tool that trainers use to train behavior is a target. Targets are often made of buoys attached to the ends of long poles. At first the cetacean is taught to simply touch the target with its head. When it has learned to touch the target, the trainer teaches it to follow the target. Once the animal is following the target regularly, the trainer can begin to shape a variety of other behaviors.

For instance, to teach a dolphin to jump out of the water, the target is put just a little bit above the surface. When the dolphin touches the target it is rewarded. Over a period of time (sometimes weeks or months) the target is gradually raised higher and higher above the surface until the dolphin is jumping all the way out of the water.

If the trainer wants to teach the dolphin to do a forward somersault in the air, he or she uses the target to shape this behavior. At the top of the dolphin's jump, the trainer moves the target in a quick clockwise circle. By following the target with its head, the dolphin does a forward somersault.

When the cetacean clearly understands a behavior and performs it consistently, the target is removed. In its place the trainer uses a hand signal to elicit the behavior, which the cetacean learns very quickly.

Once several behaviors have been learned, they are put together in a sequence called a chain. Chained behaviors are best taught backward starting with the final behavior and working toward the beginning behavior. For instance, when training a dog to retrieve, you first teach it to pick up the object and hold it in its mouth. Next you teach the dog to come to you with the object, and finally you teach it to go to the object.

Trainers try to make their training sessions as interesting as possible for their animals. They usually work on several behaviors during each session so the animals don't get bored. And trainers always end their training sessions on a positive note. If the cetacean does a behavior particularly well, the trainer rewards the animal and either moves on to the next behavior or ends the training session right there. Ending on a success like this keeps both the trainer and the cetacean motivated.

Consistency, the ability to accurately see what is going on, and good timing are the hallmarks of a good animal trainer.

In the next chapter we'll take a close look at some of the more common cetaceans kept in zoos and oceanariums.

5

A bottle-nosed dolphin.

Cetaceans in the Zoo Ark

Whales, dolphins, and porpoises come in all shapes and sizes. Here are some of the cetaceans most likely to be found in zoos and oceanariums.

Bottle-nosed dolphin · The Pacific and Atlantic bottle-nosed dolphin is the most common cetacean kept by zoos and oceanariums. It gets the name *bottle-nosed* from its well-defined snout, or beak, which extends a little over 3 inches (7.6 centimeters) from its forehead. The Pacific bottle-nosed dolphin is about 7 feet (2 meters) long. The Atlantic bottle-nosed dolphin can measure 12 feet (4 meters). Depending on the species, bottle-nosed dolphins weigh between 330 and 450 pounds (150–204 kilograms).

In the wild the bottle-nosed dolphin is found in small social groups of 2 to 15 animals. It lives mainly in coastal waters and is often seen in bays and lagoons. The dolphin's natural diet consists primarily of bottom fish. Dolphins have been known to hunt cooperatively. In captivity, bottle-nosed dolphins are fed a variety of fish and eat between 15 and 20 pounds (7–9 kilograms) a day.

In zoos and oceanariums, bottle-nosed dolphins are kept in small groups. The number of animals in the group depends on the size of the pool. Usually the largest adult male dolphin is the dominant animal in the pool, and the largest female dominates the other females. Dolphins can be aggressive toward each other. Keepers pay close attention to how the group is getting along. If there is a problem between animals, they are separated before a serious injury results.

Female bottle-nosed dolphins do not have young until they are at least 5 years old. The gestation period is 12 months. At birth, a baby bottle-nosed dolphin weighs 20 to 25 pounds (7–11 kilograms) and is 3 to 4 feet (about 1 meter) in length. The baby nurses from its mother for 12 to 18 months, but may start eating fish at 6 months. The bottle-nosed dolphin breeds very well in captivity.

Bottle-nosed dolphins are still relatively abundant in the wild. In the past they have been hunted for meat, fertilizer, and oil for cooking and lamps. They also produce a special jaw oil that was used as a lubricant in watches and precision instruments. Although most commercial dolphin fisheries have been stopped, dolphins are still caught and eaten in West Africa, Sri Lanka, Indonesia, and Japan.

Perhaps the greatest threat facing the bottle-nosed dolphin today is the tuna-fishing industry. Occasionally, dolphins get tangled in tuna nets and drown. And there have been reports of fishermen shooting dolphins in the mistaken belief that dolphins threaten their livelihood by eating the fish.

White-sided dolphin · Another dolphin commonly kept by zoos is the white-sided dolphin. It has a dark back with white stripes running along its side. The white-sided dolphin is slightly smaller than the Pacific bottle-nosed dolphin, weighing 180 to 275 pounds (82–125 kilograms) and measuring 6 or 7 feet (about 2 meters) in length. In the wild, white-sided dolphins live in groups of 6 to 15 animals, but groups of up to 1,000 animals have been seen feeding on large schools of fish. In oceanariums they are kept in small groups, often in the same pool with other cetaceans, like bottle-nosed dolphins. In captivity they are fed like bottle-nosed dolphins and eat about 15 pounds (7 kilograms) of fish a day.

White-sided dolphins are known for their great acrobatic skills. One species, the Pacific white-sided dolphin, is the only dolphin known to turn complete somersaults in the wild.

Female white-sided dolphins give birth to a single youngster after a gestation period of 10 to 12 months. The newborns average 25 pounds (11 kilograms) and are about 2.5 feet (1 meter) long. Only four white-sided dolphins have been born in captivity.

White-sided dolphins are still being caught by fishermen off the coast of Peru. The meat is sold in the markets of Lima for a little over two dollars a pound. It is estimated that 10,000 white-sided dolphins are caught and sold for meat every year. Fishermen in Japan, Newfoundland, Norway, and the British Isles are also catching these dolphins. Like the bottle-nosed dolphin, white-sided dolphins also become tangled in tuna-fishing nets and drown.

*A white-sided dolphin soars through
the air in an indoor oceanarium.*

Killer whale · Despite its name the killer whale is actually a dolphin, not a whale. It is called a whale because of its great size. Adults can reach lengths of 30 feet (9 meters) and can weigh up to 20,000 pounds (9,000 kilograms). In the wild they are found in all the oceans of the world from the Arctic to the Antarctic. They seem to prefer to stay near coastal areas, often hunting in shallow bays, estuaries, and the mouths of rivers.

Killer whales are strikingly beautiful animals. The upper parts of their bodies are black, and the lower parts are white. In the center of their backs is a large triangular dorsal fin that can reach 6 feet (2 meters) in length. They also have white patches on their flanks and on the sides of their heads. No two killer whales have the exact same patches. Researchers studying them in the wild are able to tell them apart by the different patterns.

The killer whale is no more a killer than you or I; it is simply a carnivore like dolphins, wolves, cats, and humans. The name *killer* may have been given to it because it is the only dolphin known to regularly prey on other warm-blooded mammals. In the wild, killer whales eat fish, seals, walrus, penguins, and sea turtles. They have even been known to eat other cetaceans. If a killer whale detects a bird or seal sitting near the edge of the ice in Arctic water, it may take a deep dive and rush to the surface, breaking the ice. This knocks the animal into water, where the whale snaps it up. On the Argentine coast, killer whales have been seen beaching themselves on land in order to drive resting seals into the water where they can be eaten. They have also been known to take seals right off the beach. Obviously, in captivity killer whales cannot be fed warm-blooded mammals. Instead, they are fed fish—up to 125 pounds (57 kilograms) a day!

In the wild, killer whales live in family groups called pods of about ten animals of different ages. These pods are generally well organized and led by a large male.

Killer whales adjust very well to captivity and seem to enjoy being trained and performing in shows. They are kept in small groups, usually made up of a male and two or three females.

Individual killer whales have given birth to 19 calves in captivity. The gestation period is about 17 months. When the baby is born it weighs nearly 400 pounds (181 kilograms) and measures about 7 feet (2 meters) long. The baby is weaned from its mother's milk when it is 14 to 18 months old.

Harbor porpoise · The main difference between porpoises and dolphins is that porpoises have a blunter snout and rather stocky, compact bodies. The most commonly seen porpoise in zoos and oceanariums is the harbor porpoise (also known as the common porpoise).

Harbor porpoises are found throughout the world in coastal waters, bays, estuaries, and in the mouths of large rivers. They are quite a bit smaller than dolphins, weighing from 90 to 130 pounds (41–59 kilograms), and reach a maximum length of about 5 feet (1.5 meters).

Although the harbor porpoise has been seen in groups as large as 100 animals, it is usually found in pairs or small groups of 5 to 10 animals. In the wild, it eats a variety of fish including, herring, pollack, mackerel, and sardines. In captivity, depending on its size, it is fed between 7 and 10 pounds (3–5 kilograms) of fish a day.

The harbor porpoise is not known for jumping out of the water in the wild, but in captivity it is a very accomplished jumper and acrobat. It is often kept in the same pool with other cetaceans such as dolphins and beluga whales, and it is known for its ability to swim circles around these cetaceans because of its great speed and agility. While being chased it has been known to reach speeds of 15 miles an hour (13 knots).

Not much is known about the reproduction of harbor porpoises. Few have been kept or been born in captivity. The gestation period is an estimated 10 to 11 months. Stranded newborn harbor porpoises have been raised in oceanariums. At birth the babies weigh between 13 and 17 pounds (6–8 kilograms) and average a little under 3 feet (0.9 meter) in length. In the wild, youngsters nurse from their mothers for about 8 months.

The harbor porpoise is still killed for its meat in a few countries. Off the coast of Greenland 700 to 1,500 animals are killed every year, and in Peru 250,000 pounds (113,400 kilograms) of harbor porpoise meat is marketed every year.

Beluga whale · The beluga whale is found in the Arctic Ocean, the Sea of Okhotsk, the Bering Sea, the Gulf of

Alaska, Hudson Bay, and the Gulf of St. Lawrence. It is also called a white whale because of its light-gray to white color. Females can weigh 3,000 pounds (1,360 kilograms) and reach lengths of 13 feet (4 meters). Males are slightly bigger, weighing up to 3,300 pounds (1,500 kilograms) and reaching 15 feet (5 meters) in length.

Beluga whales live in groups of about ten animals, which seem to be led by a large male. Congregations of 10,000 whales have been seen swimming up rivers to feed on schools of fish.

These whales are known for their ability to make a variety of high-pitched audible sounds while following ships and boats. For this reason they are sometimes called sea canaries.

They are not able to have young until they are six or seven years old. So far, only six beluga whales have been born in captivity. Beluga calves weigh about 175 pounds (79 kilograms) when they are born and are about 5 feet (1.5 meters) long. At birth they are gray, gradually turning lighter as they get older. The calf isn't weaned until it is about two years old. Beluga whales adapt quite well to captivity and are easily trained.

In the past, the beluga whale was an important resource for the people of the Arctic. The meat was eaten by humans and fed to dogs. The thick blubber layer was turned into oil and was used in making soap, lubricants, and margarine. The bones were ground up for fertilizer, and the skin was used to make boots and laces.

Of course, the beluga whale is no longer used this way because the Arctic people have access to other kinds of foods and supplies.

A beluga whale floats near its trainer in a moment of relaxation—or in anticipation of getting that fish on the trainer's chest.

Helping to protect the future of at least one cetacean: A keeper stays in the pool with a stranded baby porpoise until he is sure it can swim on its own.

The beluga whale population is stable. It is estimated that there are between 62,000 and 88,000 worldwide.

Will cetaceans survive? · Whether cetaceans will survive or not depends on how we treat our planet. When we pollute our oceans with sewage, industrial waste, and oil, we destroy the cetaceans' home and kill their food.

Whales, dolphins, and porpoises are very intelligent and unique animals. We are lucky to share the world with them. The question is: Are we intelligent enough to protect them?

Glossary

adaptations. Any physical or behavioral characteristics that help an animal survive in its environment.

algae. Various one-celled aquatic plants lacking stems, roots, and leaves.

anesthetize. To chemically induce a state whereby the animal loses all (or partial) physical sensation so it does not feel pain during surgery and other medical procedures.

antibiotics. Any of various substances, such as penicillin, that are used to kill microorganisms that cause disease.

behavior. Any action or reaction in response to an outside stimulus or circumstance.

buoyancy. The capacity to remain floating on the water's surface.

carnivore. An animal belonging to the scientific order Carnivora that feeds primarily on the flesh of other animals.

cetaceans. Marine mammals belonging to the scientific order Cetacea, including whales, dolphins, and porpoises.

gestation period. The period of time a female carries her offspring in the uterus before birth. Pregnancy.

husbandry. The art of caring for animals in captivity.

metabolism. The rate at which the body uses fuel or the processes associated with the body. *Metabolism* is the name for the whole working process of the body.

reinforcement. A stimulus (positive or negative), such as food or a tug on a leash, given to an animal for performing a certain behavior.

sonar. A system using transmitted and reflected sound waves to detect and locate submerged objects. Also known as echolocation.

stranders. Marine mammals that have run aground onto a beach or shore and are incapable of returning to the water on their own.

Further Reading

Coffey, David J. *Dolphins, Whales, and Porpoises: An Encyclopedia of Sea Mammals*. New York: Macmillan, 1977.

Dobbs, Horace. *Follow the Wild Dolphins*. New York: St. Martin's Press, 1988.

Gormley, Gerard. *Orcas of the Gulf*. San Francisco: Sierra Club, 1990.

Haley, Delphine, ed. *Marine Mammals*. Florence, OR: Pacific Search, 1978.

Jeune, Paul. *The Whale Who Wouldn't Die*. Chicago: Follet, 1979.

Mallory, Kenneth, and Conley, Andrea. *Rescue of the Stranded Whales*. New York: Simon and Schuster, 1989.

Norris, Kenneth. *The Porpoise Watcher*. New York: Norton, 1974.

O'Barry, Richard. *Behind the Dolphin Smile*. Chapel Hill, NC: Algonquin, 1988.

Patent, Dorothy Hinshaw. *Whales, Giants of the Deep*. New York: Holiday House, 1984.

Pryor, Karen. *Lads Before the Wind: Adventures in Porpoise Training*. New York: Harper & Row, 1975.

Scheffer, Victor B. *The Year of the Whale*. New York: Scribner's, 1969.

Scheffer, Victor B. *A Natural History of Marine Mammals*. New York: Scribner's, 1976.

Whitehead, Hal. *Voyage to the Whales*. Post Mills, VT: Chelsea Green, 1990.

Index

Page numbers in *italics* refer
to illustrations.

First You Steal 2 Eggs:

123

Delicious Recipes

& Spicy Stories

Relished by

a Happy Cooker

HEDDA HENDRIX

A FIBONACCI PRODUCTION

DISTRIBUTED BY MEDIA/AMERICA, WASHINGTON, D.C.

Text Editor: Wendy B. Murphy
Designer: Mary Ann Joulwan
Copy Editor: Kaari Ward

First Edition
Standard Book Number: 0915494-03-5
Library of Congress Catalog Number: 75-6013

To Maryout Mammott
Good Luck

To men and women of all ages
I dedicate these succulent pages.

For Saul—one personal note I must add,
You're the dearest male-chauvinist-guinea-pig
A woman ever had.

H.H.

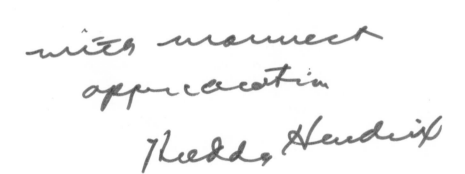

with warmest
appreciation

Thedda Hendrix

FOREWORD

"There is no spectacle on earth more appealing than that of a beautiful woman in the act of cooking dinner for someone she loves."

—Thomas Wolfe in The Web and the Rock

"Cooking dinner is like love. It should be entered into with abandon or not at all." *—Harriet Van Horne,* Vogue, *October 15, 1956*

"No mean person can cook well. It calls for a generous spirit, a light hand, and a large heart." *—A.M., in* The Irish Digest

"Foods are like words. They are for everyone. Only the cook is the poet."

—Raymond Oliver, owner of the Grand Vefour, Paris,
in an article in Marie-Claire
September, 1974

"Good recipes are like manna. They should be spread around to make things glow."   —*The author*

What do *you* want from food? Energy? Emotional satisfaction? Sex substitutes? Palate pleasure? Visual delights? Mother's love? Upward mobility and social success? Or simple nourishment. Whatever way you look at food, it's likely to play a big part in your life. So why not add a little zest to its preparation?

The making of good food is a skill that can be developed. Some people come to it naturally, and others acquire the art with training, habit and discipline. Whatever route you take, the pleasures you derive are all yours. Cooking is a universal expression of love—and as twice-blessed as "the gentle rain from heaven." From the simplest bowl of wild strawberries to a concoction aflame with brandied cherries—the range of delights is limitless. I trust that these pages will successfully communicate my enthusiasm.

CONTENTS

INTRODUCTION

Q: *How do you make an Albanian omelet?*
A: *First you steal 2 eggs:*

> One may laugh at the peasant whose only recourse
> Is a stealthy approach direct to the source,
> Or berate a poacher who steals fat rabbits.
> Away with all such felonious habits!

Here are instructions far more expedient,
Without any need for a stolen ingredient.
From many sources this collection is built,
To delight you without a *soupçon* of guilt.

> It may appear frivolous, writing light rhymes,
> But good innovations come during bad times.
> Fashions in food can change like the weather,
> You may eat much less, but enjoy it far better.

Learning to cook is like any fine art
If you heed good advice right at the start.
Work on clear surfaces, use well-scrubbed pots,
Wash vegetables clean to avoid little what-nots.

> Read every recipe from beginning to end,
> Then carefully shop with the money you spend.
> Bring out the ingredients and utensils you need,
> Arrange them nearby to cook with more speed.

Measure each quantity—be kind to yourself,
Return the ingredient back to the shelf.
You'll avoid messy spills if you're accident prone,
You won't get in trouble if you answer the phone.

Arrange the table with your prettiest service,
Whether simple or fancy, no need to get nervous.
Leave counters clear in a kitchen not spacious,
To pile up soiled dishes while you remain gracious.

Recipes are ordered to help you select
Interesting foods you could often neglect.
Don't worry at all about getting fat,
There's quite a simple solution for that.

Give up the boring calorie count,
Help yourself to a smaller amount.
The Chinese and Indians, to avoid any gluttony,
Stay slim on rice and a bit of chutney.

All recipes were tested, you need have no fear,
Measurements "on the level" make everything clear.
Where suited you'll find a suggestion for wine,
To add to your pleasure whenever you dine.

First
You Steal
2
Eggs:

1

CRACK EGGS WITH STYLE

You can scramble, coddle, bake, or fry them,
You can poach, paint, or color-dye them.
Perfectly formed to amuse or beguile,
Here are 14 ways to crack eggs with style.

Use the yolks for Mayonnaise or to thicken a broth.
Whip up the whites till they form a stiff froth.
The Meringue or Soufflé will rise to perfection
When you follow the HOW TO for each recipe selection.

WHOLE EGGS:

TWO-ON-A-RAFT

This is the first dish I ever cooked, and it continues to be a wonderful way to prepare eggs and toast without a toaster. I learned how to make it on a canoe trip when I was ten years old, and for me it is still the handiest method of fixing the popular breakfast combination. What's more, everything is ready at the same time. Serves 1.

2 eggs
2 slices of white, rye,
  or whole wheat bread
2 tablespoons butter
Salt and pepper to taste

HOW TO: Make a hole about the size of a 50-cent piece in the center of each slice of bread. Butter the bread on both sides and place in a frying pan over low heat. Drop ¼ teaspoon of butter in the center of each hole so the yolk won't stick. Carefully break an egg over each slice of bread so the yolk drops into the hole. Fry the bread a few minutes until the whites set. Then add a little butter to the pan, flip the bread, and fry another few minutes until the yokes are firm, but not hard. Sprinkle with salt and pepper.

IRISH ROASTIES

For camping indoors before the fireplace, here's an interesting alternative to roasting potatoes or toasting marshmallows. Children will enjoy the experience, and high-protein dieters can partake of the pleasures, too.

  I discovered the recipe while browsing through The Art of Irish Cookery *by Monica Sheridan. She describes it among her many childhood memories, adding a bit of Gaelic wisdom; "Ubh han salann, pog gan croimbeal." Translation: "An egg without salt is like a kiss from a beardless man."*

Eggs, at least 1 per person
Hot wood or coal ashes
  (not embers) in the fireplace
Salt

HOW TO: Pierce the top of each egg with a pin to enable the sulphur fumes to escape during the roasting. Place upright in the warm ashes for half an hour, then rake out. Remove the shells and sprinkle the eggs with salt. They should be quite hard and have a most unusual flavor.

MANDARIN EGGS

These eggs are easy appetizers to serve at home and convenient to take along on a picnic because no salt is needed, the soy sauce supplies enough flavor. I found these in Hong Kong. Serves 4.

4 eggs, 1 per person
3 tablespoons soy sauce
1 tablespoon vegetable oil

HOW TO: Boil the eggs in their shells for about 6 minutes until hard. Cool and crack under cold water and remove the shells. Place the whole shelled eggs in a small saucepan. Combine the soy sauce and vegetable oil and add to the pan. Cook for about 5 minutes over moderate heat, rotating the eggs until they become medium brown all over. Allow to cool in the sauce, then refrigerate. When fairly cold, cut the eggs in half lengthwise. The whites will have shaded from brown outside to beige inside for a very appealing effect.

TASTI ZAKUSKI

This is a fine hors d'oeuvre, salad, or main luncheon dish. I use it as a dinner prelude when I serve my Godunov Borscht (see recipe on page 33). Kay Shaw Nelson, a noted cooking authority of Washington, D.C., is my source for this zakuski — the word for appetizer in Polish. Allow 2 eggs per person. Serves 4.

8 eggs
¼ cup sour cream
2 tablespoons chives or green onions, finely chopped

2 tablespoons fresh dill or parsley, finely chopped
Salt and pepper to taste
Paprika

HOW TO: Boil the eggs in their shells for about 6 minutes until hard. Cool and crack under cold water and remove the shells. Cut the eggs lengthwise into halves. Remove the yolks and mash. Mix with the sour cream, chives or onions, dill or parsley, salt, and pepper. Stuff the egg white halves with the mixture and sprinkle with paprika. Chill. Serve on a bed of fresh, crisp greens and enhance with *crudités* (raw vegetable slices), depending upon the occasion.

NO-YEAST COFFEE CAKE

For genuine hospitality, there is nothing like a homemade cake to serve with fresh-brewed coffee. It fills the house with fragrant odors during the baking process, suffusing heart and hearth with good feelings.

Mrs. Lane Bryant, founder of the national chain of stores catering to special sizes and the creator of the original maternity dress, was a dear and valued family friend. She ran a large household with a generous table. Lane Bryant was more concerned with the nourishing qualities of the food than with fancy presentation. Among the many memories I have of her generosity to me—from childhood birthday gifts to graduation and wedding presents—is this treasured recipe.

Because No-Yeast Coffee Cake takes exactly 15 minutes to assemble and pop into the oven, I bake it frequently. It's ideal for breakfast gatherings and will raise eyebrows—as well as consciousness—at your skill. It helps me resist commercial cakes, as I know it is easy, cheaper, and more satisfying than anything I could buy—even at today's prices. Yields 16 2-inch cubes at a mere 10 cents a serving.

¼ pound (1 stick) sweet butter
¾ cup sugar
2 eggs, unbeaten
1 cup sour cream
1 teaspoon vanilla extract
1¾ cups all-purpose flour
1½ teaspoons baking powder

½ teaspoon baking soda
1 teaspoon cinnamon
3 tablespoons sugar
2 tablespoons currants or raisins
2 tablespoons walnuts or pecans, chopped
(the above 4 should total ½ cup)

14

HOW TO: Preheat oven to 350° F. Beat the butter and ¾ cup of sugar together, add the eggs and mix well. Blend in the sour cream and vanilla extract. Sift together the flour, baking powder, and baking soda, then add to the butter and egg mixture. Beat about a minute or until all the ingredients are well blended. In a square (8"x 8"), well-greased pan, place half the dough and sprinkle with ¼ cup of the cinnamon-sugar-raisin-nut mixture. Cover with the remaining dough, and top with the remaining ¼ cup of blended nut-sugar mixture. Bake for 45 minutes till toothpick test shows it's done. Cut into 2-inch squares to serve.

EGG YOLKS

SUPA VES LIMUA

The Albanians, like the Greeks, are addicted to a flavorful, rich light soup that is an excellent first course. The soup may be partially prepared beforehand, but the egg yolks and lemon juice must be added just before it is served. This is another find from the collection of Kay Shaw Nelson. Serves 6 to 8.

2 quarts chicken broth	**Salt and pepper**
½ cup uncooked rice	**Juice of 2 lemons**
1 tablespoon butter or margarine	**2 teaspoons fresh mint, chopped**
2 egg yolks, beaten	

HOW TO: In a large saucepan bring the broth to a boil. Add the rice and lower heat. Cook slowly, covered, until the rice is tender, about 20 minutes. Stir in the butter or margarine. Season with salt and pepper. In a separate dish combine the egg yolks and lemon juice. Pour a little hot soup into the yolk and lemon-juice mixture. Add to the remaining soup, leave over low heat, stirring constantly, 2 to 3 minutes. Serve at once. Do not reheat. Garnish with chopped mint.

15

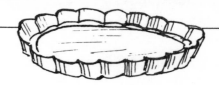

CRACKING A CORDON BLEU MYSTERY

Time: 6 P.M., Tuesday evening, mid-July
Setting: The kitchen-cum-breakfast nook in the Whelan's home in Chappaqua, a lush green suburban town 40 miles north of New York City
Characters: Jeannette Whelan, wife of the architect-owner; Lynda Whelan Kilburn, her daughter, mother of two time-consuming toddlers, on a visit from Norfolk, Connecticut. Me, the author.

Jeannette and I sip chilled white wine to keep cool while awaiting the arrival of our husbands. Lynda, standing at the kitchen counter, pops a ready-made pie crust into the oven, then casually starts to dice some Swiss cheese, chop an onion, and grill a few slices of bacon in a skillet.

Me: "Looks as if you are ready to feed the children. What are you making for them?"
Lynda: "They've eaten already—I'm making a Quiche Au Fromage for *our* supper."

My interest was piqued, for I was on the threshold of a great breakthrough. The mysterious quiche, which I had enjoyed at catered cocktail parties, but had dismissed as too complicated for my own amateur's repertoire! Surely, I thought, it required lengthy preparation and utensils that were strangers to my kitchen.

To my astonishment, Quiche Au Fromage turned out to be just a simple combination of cheese, eggs, and cream with some tasty tidbits of onion and bacon, all baked in an open pie shell.

I have never since been awed by any "complicated" dish. Lynda's procedures had revealed the simple know-how to crack one cordon bleu secret. Soon after, I tackled a crêpe, ventured a mousse, and finally whipped up enough yolks, whites—and courage—to make a soufflé. These dishes were all only more beautiful ways to glorify eggs—fancy fixings with a bit of fuss, far easier to make than many of the long-winded instructional cookbooks had led me to believe.

Moral: By hanging around other people's kitchens you may be privy to some well-kept culinary secrets.

QUICHE AU FROMAGE

A ready-frozen pastry shell is a handy item to keep in one's freezer for preparing quick meals. Serves 4 to 6 as a main course or 8 as an hors d'oeuvre.

¼ **pound bacon (6 strips)**
½ **cup onion, coarsely chopped**
1 **9-inch pie crust, homemade or ready-frozen**
½ **pound Swiss cheese, diced into ½-inch cubes**

2 **eggs, lightly beaten**
1 **cup milk or half-and-half or light cream (the heavier, the richer)**
½ **teaspoon salt**
Pinch of cayenne pepper
Pinch of nutmeg

HOW TO: Preheat oven to 450° F. In a skillet fry the bacon until crisp. Drain on a paper towel. Coarsely crumble the bacon and set aside. In 1 tablespoon of bacon fat, cook the onion slowly until golden brown. Place the pastry-lined 9-inch pie pan or a 9-inch oven-to-table quiche dish in the oven. Bake for 5 minutes. Remove from the oven and add the bacon, onions, and cheese. Mix together the eggs, milk, and seasonings. Pour into the pie crust and bake for 10 minutes. Reduce heat to 325° F. and continue to bake for about 20 minutes, or until firm. Use toothpick to test for doneness.

SUMMER SALMON MOUSSE

I am not a devotee of aspics and such, but this salmon dish is an exception. Made in a ceramic or copper fish form, it is most appetizing to look at. This takes only 2 yolks, leaving you 2 egg whites to make the Date Kisses or Almond Macaroons offered later in this chapter.

Margery Harrison of Briarcliff, New York, is my source for this cool dish. It is one she treasures from her mother and came to me as a reward for solving an elusive word in The New York Times *crossword puzzle. (Margery and I share a common passion for Sunday puzzles.)*

It is a wonderful summer dish, a fine change from the usual cold poached salmon. Make it a day ahead of time or early in the morning. The cucumber sauce is a cinch, too. (See color photograph on page 74.) Serves 6 to 8.

1 packet unflavored gelatin	¾ cup scalded milk
¼ cup cold water	1½ tablespoons butter, melted
1 pound canned salmon	2 egg yolks, beaten
½ tablespoon salt	2 tablespoons cold water
1½ tablespoons sugar	¼ cup hot vinegar
1 teaspoon dry mustard	

Dill

Sauce
1 cup sour cream
1 cucumber, peeled, seeded,
  and finely chopped

2 tablespoons fresh dill
  or chives, finely chopped
Black pepper to taste

HOW TO: Soften the gelatin in ¼ cup of cold water. Rinse the salmon in cold water and drain thoroughly. Remove any skin or bones, pick the flesh clean and break into fine pieces. Set aside. Add the salt, sugar, and mustard to the scalded milk. Mix well in the top of a double boiler and cook over low heat for 5 minutes, stirring constantly—do not boil. To this add the melted butter, egg yolks (which have been beaten with 2 tablespoons of cold water), and hot vinegar. Stir and cook 1 minute longer. Add the softened gelatin and stir until it dissolves. Add the minced salmon and blend all together. Turn into a very lightly oiled fish mold. Refrigerate for 4 hours, or until firm.

To unmold, gently place the mold in a pan of lukewarm water for a minute and then turn it upside down onto an oblong serving platter. Encircle the mousse with watercress, parsley, or lettuce.

To make the cucumber sauce, mix the sour cream with cucumber. Sprinkle with dill or chives and top with freshly ground black pepper. Serve in a separate bowl for individual helpings.

SUGGESTED WINE: ANJOU ROSÉ (SEMIDRY PINK LOIRE)

GOLDEN MAYONNAISE

Like Summer Salmon Mousse, preceding page, this recipe needs only the yolks of 2 eggs, so make it in conjunction with something that uses up the white, and you will feel smugly economical. The trick in making good mayonnaise is to add the oil so slowly that the yolks absorb it. The electric blender is a perfect tool for this, as it leaves both hands free to deal with the yolks. An electric beater works well, too, but takes much more time.

A little curry powder or white pepper may be added to suit your taste. For vinegar, I prefer the tarragon-flavored variety. Yields 1 cup.

2 egg yolks	**1 teaspoon salt**
2 teaspoons vinegar or lemon juice	**2 teaspoons sugar**
½ teaspoon dry mustard	**1 cup salad oil**

HOW TO: Place the yolks and all the other ingredients except the oil into the blender. Add ¼ cup of the salad oil, cover, and run the machine for about 5 seconds. Without stopping the machine, remove the cover and slowly add the remaining ¾ cup of the oil in a fine, thin stream. Stop the machine when last of the oil is blended. If the mayonnaise is not thick enough, pour into the top of a double boiler and whisk over hot water, about 5 minutes, to cook the yolks. You can thin it with a bit of sour cream or fruit juice, depending on what you plan to serve. Store in a tightly covered jar in the refrigerator. It will last a week or two, at most.

EGG WHITES:

DATE KISSES

Jo Pomerance of Cos Cob, Connecticut, a political scientist and writer, provides this little bon bouche *for her guests' delectation. I asked Briged Genovese, her competent cook, for the recipe. What a surprise to discover that these chewy delights required only 1 egg white. This provides a fine way to whip a lone leftover white into a whole batch of handy sweets. Makes about 4 dozen.*

1 egg white
1 cup confectioners' sugar
1 pound of pitted dates, finely chopped
1 cup slivered, blanched almonds

HOW TO: Preheat oven to 325° F. Beat the egg white until stiff. Blend in the sugar. Add the dates and almonds. Mix well. Drop by heaping teaspoonfuls onto a lightly greased cookie sheet. Bake 20 to 25 minutes until lightly browned. Remove from the oven and with a spatula quickly lift cookies onto a serving dish. Do not store in a closed cookie jar.

ALMOND MACAROONS

A most satisfactory way to use 2 egg whites is this popular flavored cookie. It requires no flour, butter, or milk. The almond paste may be found in most food shops that handle imports. This is my mother's recipe, and I have added the pine nuts for a more sophisticated look. Makes about 2 dozen.

½ pound almond paste
  (available in 12-ounce cans)
1 cup plus 2 tablespoons
  fine sugar (Superfine)

2 egg whites, lightly beaten
1 tablespoon pine nuts
Vegetable oil

HOW TO: Preheat oven to 325° F. Combine the almond paste with the sugar and egg whites. Work the mixture well until free of all lumps. Line a shallow cookie pan (10" x 14") with brown paper (a grocery bag, cut to fit, is fine) and oil the paper. Put the dough into a pastry tube and make into rounds about 1 inch in size, or shape with a spoon. Place rounds 2 inches apart to give them room to spread. Dot each macaroon with a pine nut. Bake for about 15 to 20 minutes. Remove from the oven and lift the macaroons from the paper before they are completely cooled onto a serving dish.

**YOLKS & WHITES
SEPARATED:**

UNFORGETTABLE LEMON TORTE

When you feel flush with 5 whole eggs or have 5 separated yolks and 5 separated whites stored away, you can use your hoarded treasure for the most lemony-flavored dessert I know—a light, fluffy accompaniment to Sybil Hartfield's Bouillabaisse (see recipe on page 68).

This torte is the creation of a famous Beverly Hills hostess, Sally Gluck. She is well known for interesting buffet dinners.

The original name was "Forgotten Torte," because the meringue shell is made a full 24 hours in advance, popped into a heated oven, and then, with the heat turned off, "forgotten" there. Don't plan to use your oven for any other purpose while the meringue is slowly taking shape.

An electric beater is necessary for making the meringue, as it gets very thick in the beating process. Use an 8-inch springform pan. Serves 6.

Meringue Shell
5 egg whites
¼ **teaspoon salt**
½ **teaspoon cream of tartar**

1 ½ **cups sugar**
1 **teaspoon vanilla extract**

HOW TO: Preheat oven to 425° F. for ½ hour. Beat the egg whites until frothy, but not stiff. Sprinkle the salt and the cream of tartar on top. Continue beating the eggs, gradually adding the sugar, 2 tablespoons at a time, until the mixture becomes stiff. Add the vanilla extract. Lightly spoon the meringue into a well-greased 8-inch spring-form pan. Cover the bottom with about a ½-inch-thick layer and then pile the remaining meringue on the outer edges to create a 2-inch-high border. *Turn off the heat in the oven. Place the meringue on the center shelf of the oven. Leave it overnight—a full 24 hours. Do not peek.*

Lemon Filling

  5 egg yolks
¾ cup sugar
  4 tablespoons lemon juice

2 tablespoons grated lemon rind
1 pint heavy cream, whipped
  (diet whip can be substituted)

HOW TO: Beat the yolks until thick and lemon colored. Gradually beat in the sugar. Blend in the lemon juice and rind. Place the mixture in the top of a double boiler and cook over hot water, stirring constantly, until thick, about 5 to 8 minutes. Let cool. Put one-half of the whipped cream on the meringue layer. Fold another 3 tablespoons into the lemon mixture and fill the meringue torte. You can pipe the remaining whipped cream around the top edge for an elegant look.

GINGER SOUFFLÉ

Some women dream of breakfast at Tiffany's, but I spend hours fantasying about lunch and dinner treats while browsing through La Cuisinière, the Tiffany of all New York kitchen accessory shops. Mr. J. H. Chichester, the owner of this unique Madison Avenue emporium, travels the world over collecting a marvelous array of antique and modern molds, platters, forms, pots, pans, and assorted gadgets that you seldom find elsewhere. We recipe-chat frequently. When I bought my first soufflé dish from him he graciously gave me this recipe.

I am a ginger lover, and if you, too, find that special taste irresistible, you will appreciate this recipe. It's a rare discovery. Making a soufflé is not so mysterious, just read the instructions carefully and you can quietly sneak up on it once you realize that it's only a simple white sauce enhanced by flavoring and eggs. Use a 1½-quart soufflé dish. Serves 6.

6 tablespoons butter
6 tablespoons flour
1½ cups milk
5 eggs, separated

½ cup candied crystallized
 ginger, chopped
½ cup sugar

HOW TO: Preheat oven to 450° F. To prepare the soufflé dish, grease bottom and sides well with butter and sprinkle with a little sugar. Set aside in the refrigerator before preparing the soufflé mixture.

In a saucepan, over low heat, melt the butter and flour to make a roux. Blend until smooth. In another saucepan gently warm the milk. Add the milk to the flour and butter mixture. Beat until smooth and bring to a simmer over low heat. Add the chopped candied ginger and sugar. Mix until the ginger is well blended. *Let cool. This is a most important step in making a successful soufflé.* To do this, transfer the mixture from the still-hot saucepan into a bowl. It speeds up the process.

Add the egg yolks one at a time, stirring well after each addition.

In a separate bowl whip the egg whites until they form soft peaks, and with a wooden spoon fold them little by little into the mixture. Pour into the soufflé dish and bake 30 minutes until the top is a rich brown. Turn off the heat. You may let the soufflé rest for about 5 minutes before serving.

The soufflé should be light and delicate and slightly moist in the center. However, if you prefer a firmer center, cook 10 minutes longer.

PERFECT CHEESECAKE

For this universal favorite, you need 6 eggs, and 15 minutes to whip up the ingredients with an electric beater. Guests praise it as better than anything they've ever tasted in a restaurant or bakery at triple the price.

This creamy creation comes from Crys Gartner of Waccabuc, New York, where she reports local activities for The Patent Trader, *a Northern Westchester newspaper.*

I prefer to make it a day ahead because, as tasty as it is the first day, it gets creamier when cold. It does a great disappearing act, but if there's any left over, it freezes well. Allow it to thaw ½ hour before you serve it again. Use an 8-inch spring-form pan. Serves 12.

6 eggs, separated	1 cup sugar
3 large packages (8 ounces each) cream cheese (Philadelphia brand)	½ pint sour cream
	2 teaspoons lemon juice
	Rind of 1 lemon, grated
2 tablespoons flour	1 teaspoon vanilla extract

HOW TO: Preheat oven 325° F. Combine the egg yolks and cream cheese and beat until smooth. An electric beater will do. Add the flour, sugar, and sour cream. Beat all together thoroughly. Add the lemon juice, rind, and vanilla extract — and beat some more. In a separate bowl beat the egg whites until they stand in stiff peaks. Fold gently into the yolk and cheese mixture with a wooden spoon. Pour into an ungreased spring-form pan. Bake for 1 to 1¼ hours, or until the center appears firm. Test the center with a toothpick for firmness. The top will be broken a little, and the cheesecake will fall in the center a bit after cooling when out of the oven. That's the way it should be—don't worry. Do not remove the outer rim of the spring-form pan for at least 1 hour, or until cool.

Be A
Quick Escape
Artist

MAKE A FAST GETAWAY

Enjoy what's cooking for your supper,
Don't fret if you're the cleaner upper.
Prepare in an instant or ahead a day
To help you make a fast getaway.

Heat hors d'oeuvres, soup, or seafood dishes
Offer tasty birds to make dinner auspicious.
Veal that's a cinch, Borscht that's a find,
With Pears or Squares you'll have peace of mind.

2

CHEDDAR CHEESE AND PECAN LOG

For a hurried curried kick, here's a delectable cold hors d'oeuvre. It takes just 5 minutes to prepare, can be kept in the refrigerator for several weeks, and thawed in 15 minutes. I tasted it at a cocktail party in Ardsley, New York, and held up the hostess, Anne Lieberman, for the recipe. It tested out perfectly, so perfectly in fact that I gave the secret to The Mouse Trap, a cheese and delicacy shop in Katonah, New York, where the owners tell me it has become a great seller. Anyone who divides time between a city and country home and wants to prepare weekend delicacies in advance will find this cheese log an excellent traveler. Serve with toast rounds or unsalted crackers and let the guests help themselves. Serves 16 to 20.

1 pound sharp Cheddar cheese,
  grated, or 1 container (16 ounces)
  Wispride
1 small package (3 ounces)
  cream cheese

1 cup pecans, chopped
Dash of cayenne pepper
2 tablespoons brandy (optional)
1 clove garlic, crushed (optional)
3 tablespoons curry powder

HOW TO: Allow the cheeses to warm to room temperature. Place all the ingredients except the curry powder in a mixing bowl and blend thoroughly. Place the cheese blend on a piece of wax paper. Form it into the shape of a log, about 2 inches in diameter. Sprinkle the wax paper with curry powder and roll log lightly to coat completely—be sure also to coat the ends. Wrap in fresh wax paper and refrigerate or freeze. About 45 minutes before serving, remove the log from freezer and thaw at room temperature.

DANDY CANDIED BACON

Cocktail tempters that eliminate crumbs, toothpicks, or dishes for dips are a favorite of mine. Leave it to Evelyn Lauder of New York City to come up with this Dandy Candied Bacon. She is the wife of the president of Estée Lauder, Inc., the internationally famous cosmetics firm. Evelyn is also a busy executive concerned with the development of new products for the company. She is always on the lookout, too, for quick preparations to handle her entertaining needs at home.

Make this finger food early the same day or a day in advance, and keep in the refrigerator. Serve at room temperature when needed. At party time fill the center of a platter with a bunch of parsley and radiate the bacon strips around it. Lovely to look at and heavenly bliss! Yields 24 pieces.

12 slices lean good bacon
2 cups brownulated sugar
or regular brown sugar
6 parsley sprigs

HOW TO: Preheat oven to 375° F. Cut the bacon strips in half. Coat each half with brown sugar. Place the coated bacon strips on a rack or a metal pan to catch any fat drippings. Place in the oven and bake for 15 minutes. Be careful not to brown or burn the strips. Remove the pan from the oven and place the bacon strips on a piece of aluminum foil to cool. Do not use absorbent paper towels; the fat should not be absorbed. When cool, place the strips on a serving platter or store in the refrigerator until needed. Serve at room temperature.

SHRIMPS INDIENNE

This is a hot appetizer or entrée, depending on your pocketbook. The combination of several spices results in a very subtle taste that defies easy analysis by your guests. Sneaked by a pupil of the late Michael Field, the well-known cooking authority, it was swapped in a trade with one of my best recipes— and well worth it. Serves 5 or 6 as an entrée or 10 as an accompaniment to drinks.

1 cup vegetable oil
1 tablespoon wine vinegar, red or
white
1 teaspoon salt
1 teaspoon dried basil
2 teaspoons chili powder

1 tablespoon fresh mint, finely
chopped
2 tablespoons garlic, finely chopped
1 teaspoon lemon juice
20 large raw shrimp, shelled and
deveined with tails left on
¼ cup parsley, minced

27

HOW TO: Make a marinade of the oil, vinegar, seasonings, herbs, garlic, and lemon juice. Cover the shrimps and let stand in the marinade from ½ to 2 hours, at your convenience. When ready to serve, place all in a shallow pan under a preheated broiler about 3 inches from the source of heat and broil for approximately 5 minutes on each side. Serve in the broiling dish and top with a sprinkling of minced parsley.

SUGGESTED WINE: GEWURZTRAMINER (TANGY WHITE ALSACE) OR INDIA PALE ALE

SCALLOPS FLAMBÉE

This superb entrée came to me through a chain letter from Marjorie Webb of Greenwich, Connecticut—the only time I collected anything in quite such a serendipitous manner. It's made to order for the host or hostess who doesn't like to be a cooking schnook while the guests are amusing themselves elsewhere. A flambé in a chafing dish highlights the solo performance. Men's lib, please note: The whole deal takes about 15 minutes to prepare and 8 minutes to cook. Serves 6.

2 pints fresh bay scallops	**7 tablespoons butter**
1 cup dry white wine	**1 ½ tablespoons brandy**
½ pound fresh mushrooms, caps and stems, chopped	**½ cup heavy cream**
	Salt and pepper to taste

HOW TO: In a saucepan cook the scallops in the white wine over moderate heat for about 15 minutes. Trim and wash the mushrooms and cut into small pieces. *Ten minutes before serving,* heat the butter in a skillet, lightly sauté the mushrooms, about 2 minutes. They should remain firm. Then add the well-drained scallops. Cook for 5 or 6 minutes over moderate heat; add the brandy and ignite. When flame dies out, add the cream and seasonings. Bring to a boil and serve. This goes well with perfectly cooked rice (see recipe on page 93).

SUGGESTED WINE: JOHANNISBERG RIESLING (GERMAN RHINE OR CALIFORNIA)

ZUPPA VERDE

One can frequently date the publication of a cookbook by the recipe procedures it offers. Many instructions are now outmoded, especially the profligate ones that some writers give to "discard egg whites down the drain," or yolks, depending upon which part of the egg is used in a recipe.

These days I throw nothing away. This recipe is a perfect example of how to apply a bit of simple arithmetic, starting with something I might have tossed aside in earlier times and working out an equation with other ingredients to go with it. My husband kids me about my limited mathematical skills, to which I reply, "I may go to my grave with an unbalanced checkbook, but my refrigerator will be filled with plenty to eat for anyone who comes to my wake."

Here's a recipe I created when left with the stems of a bunch of watercress after making a salad of the leaves. Using a little poetic license, I have called this beautiful soup, which is as green as "the auld sod," Zuppa Verde. You may serve it piping hot with slivers of thinly sliced zucchini to top it off or well chilled with a spoonful of sour cream and a sprinkling of finely chopped parsley or chives. It's your choice, depending on the weather. Cheat with a bit of cream of wheat to give the soup a little body, so there's no need to use butter or flour. Yields at least 2 quarts; serves 8.

Stems from a bunch of watercress
Green tops from a bunch of scallions, chopped
6 sprigs of parsley, tops and stems, chopped
4 stalks of celery, tops and stems, chopped
2 cucumbers, peeled, seeded, chopped

1 quart water
4 cups chicken broth or 3 chicken bouillon cubes in 4 cups water
3 tablespoons uncooked cream of wheat
Pinch of seasoned salt or your favorite seasoning mixture

HOW TO: Place all the ingredients except the cream of wheat and seasonings into a 4- or 6-quart kettle. Bring to a boil and simmer over low heat for 40 minutes. Remove all the vegetables from soup to purée in a blender for about 1 minute. Return puréed mix to the liquid and add the cream of wheat and seasonings. Simmer slowly for another 5 minutes. Serve hot or cold.

PRETTY HENNY PENNY
OR THE PHONY TRUFFLED GROSBREAST

Here is a dressy way to cook chicken breasts—a dish as tasty as it is beautiful. You will find that those who normally eschew the white meat will be surprised by the succulence of chicken breasts served in this way.

To do it justice, I thought it deserved a name worthy of Audubon. I asked the noted architect Morris Ketchum, Jr., designer of the magnificent World of Birds in the Bronx Park Zoo in New York City, for the names of some rare bird species. He rattled off the names of several unusual specimens, though he cautioned they could only be seen through martini glasses. He added that these rarae aves travel in pairs; the Morning Grouse and the Ruffled Spouse, the Rosy-Breasted Pushover and the Double-Breasted Seersucker. The most famous couple sighted throughout the American landscape is the Extramarital Lark, always accompanied by the Great American Regret. This loving pair have a distinctive cry as they fly: "Kinzeeee, Kinzeeee, Kinzeeee . . ."

Thus inspired, I call this way of serving the whole stuffed breast of chicken Pretty Henny Penny or the Phony Truffled Grosbreast. Silvia Gronich, an art gallery director, introduced me to the then-unnamed recipe when she was our houseguest.

If you are fortunate enough to have a benevolent butcher, ask him to bone the breasts of the chicken without slicing them in half. They must be whole boned breasts with the skin left on. However, if your market only sells whole breasts with the bone left in, you can do the surgery at home.

To serve it hot and shorten the cleanup process, use an oven-to-table dish. To serve it cold for lunch, cut the cooked chicken into ½-inch slices, making beautiful semicircles of chicken and stuffing. The currants are thereby revealed, giving them an appearance of truffles. Garnish the cold chicken slices with nests of watercress at the last minute before serving. (See color photograph on page 75.) Serves 4 to 6 either delicious way.

30

4 boned whole chicken breasts
¼ package prepared seasoned
   bread stuffing
2 teaspoons nutmeg
¾ teaspoon powdered ginger

¼ cup dried currants
1 tablespoon parsley, finely
   chopped
3 tablespoons butter

HOW TO: Preheat oven to 375° F. Wash the chicken breasts and dry. Bone if not already done so. Prepare the packaged stuffing as directed or make your own, as preferred—it should be on the moist side. To the stuffing add 1¼ teaspoons of the nutmeg, ½ teaspoon of the ginger, the currants, and parsley. Flatten breasts, skin side down, and on each one place 4 tablespoons of the stuffing. Fold both sides toward center and then fold top and bottom toward center. Turn the chicken folded side down and place in a roasting pan, skin side up. This should make a lovely ball shape. Melt the butter and season with the remaining nutmeg and ginger. Brush skin with the seasoned butter. Bake for 40 minutes, uncovered. No additional basting is required.

SUGGESTED WINE: BERNKASTELER GREEN LABEL (MOSELLE)

CHICKEN LICKEN

This recipe is the tastiest way I know of preparing the wings, thighs, and legs of a chicken. Pretty Henny Penny, the recipe above, is good for the chicken breasts, which cook in less time to remain moist and tender.

Chicken Licken takes only 5 minutes to prepare and 45 minutes to cook, can be easily made in the morning and quickly reheated when ready to serve. It's a procedure you can personalize by adding your favorite seasonings to the bread crumbs. For example, use a combination of basil and oregano instead of ginger and cloves, or just plain paprika. You can make it any way you like and come up with a winner every time. For 4 people, use 8 to 10 chicken parts—wings, thighs, or legs.

3 pounds chicken wings, thighs
   and/or legs
¼ cup plus 1 tablespoon vegetable
   oil
½ cup unseasoned fine bread
   crumbs

¼ teaspoon salt
¼ teaspoon white pepper
½ teaspoon powdered ginger
⅛ teaspoon powdered cloves

HOW TO: Preheat oven to 325° F. Wipe the chicken parts dry. Place ¼ cup of vegetable oil in a shallow dish. Flavor the bread crumbs with all the seasonings (salt, pepper, ginger, cloves). Dip each piece of chicken in oil and then roll lightly in seasoned bread crumbs. Place coated chicken in a flat-oven-to-table dish, skin down. Sprinkle 1 tablespoon of oil over top. Cook the chicken for 45 minutes, turning once. Skin should be crisp, and if not golden brown after 45 minutes, remove from the oven and place under medium hot broiler and cook another 10 minutes before serving.

SUGGESTED WINE: MUSCADET (DRY, FRUITY WHITE LOIRE) OR CHENIN BLANC (CALIFORNIA)

VEAL PICCATA

This is ideal for a saucerer's apprentice. Its great virtues are simplicity of preparation and its brief, 10 minutes of cooking time—and it's guaranteed to elicit applause. I filched this original jewel from a friend's recipe treasure chest with her acquiescence, and reset it in my own kitchen. Serves 4.

8 to 10 scallops of veal, flattened
   but not pounded too thin
   (about 1¼ pounds)
Salt and pepper to taste
¼ cup flour
4 tablespoons butter (don't
   cheat with margarine, but
   olive oil is okay)
¼ cup dry vermouth

¼ cup beef bouillon or
½ bouillon cube in ¼ cup
   hot water
1 tablespoon fresh rosemary
   or 2 teaspoons dried
1 tablespoon scallions,
   chopped
1 tablespoon parsley, chopped
10 wafer-thin slices lemon

HOW TO: Season the tender pieces of veal with salt and pepper. Dust with flour; shake off excess. Sauté quickly on both sides in butter or oil. Add the dry vermouth and beef bouillon to the pan. Reduce sauce until thickened. Sprinkle with the rosemary, scallions, and parsley, and place a wafer-thin slice of lemon on top of each scallop. Cook gently for 2 to 3 minutes longer. Transfer to a heated serving platter or serve in cooking pan.

SUGGESTED WINE: SOAVE (DRY WHITE VERONESE)

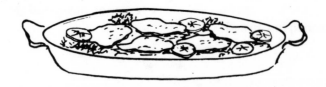

GODUNOV BORSCHT

For a hearty one-dish meal transported from Boris' steppes, try this. It's an aromatic heirloom of a Russian pianist who loved cooking shortcuts that allowed her more time to practice at the keyboard. The assembly takes 5 minutes, and the cooking requires no attention at all. It may be made at night and served the next day as a soup for the first course or as a main dish; and the best part is that you spend no time in the kitchen when you entertain guests. Leftovers are great reheated. Best in cold weather. Serves 6 generously.

1 ½ quarts cold water
4 pounds beef flanken (beef for boiling), cut into 2-inch chunks
1 ½ pounds sauerkraut, fresh or canned
1 or 2 onions, chopped
2 or 3 tablespoons sugar
1 can (12 ounces) stewed tomatoes
1 bay leaf
Salt and pepper to taste
8 small boiled potatoes, skinned
½ pint sour cream (optional)
Horseradish

HOW TO: Place all the ingredients except the potatoes and sour cream in a 4- to 6-quart kettle and cook slowly for 2 ½ hours, or "till tender." Put in a bowl to cool, then rest overnight in refrigerator. Skim the congealed fat from the top. Reheat when ready to eat. Serve the soup separately, adding a tablespoon of sour cream to each portion for the Russian touch. Add the potatoes, sauerkraut, and remaining liquid to the meat, and serve as a main dish in a casserole. For a condiment offer plain white horseradish.

SUGGESTED WINE: CORBIERES OR ROUSSILLON (FLAVORFUL RED FROM SOUTHERN FRANCE)

GINGER PEARS

This delight was purloined from writer Theresa A. Morse of Martha's Vineyard, Massachusetts, whose culinary art sustained many literary figures.

Allow 15 minutes preparation time and, if possible, do it a day or two ahead so that the flavors marry and the fruit is properly chilled. Please note: No sugar needed. Serves 6.

1 tablespoon grated orange rind
1 tablespoon grated lemon rind
3 tablespoons fresh lemon juice
½ cup fresh orange juice

2 teaspoons minced crystallized
 ginger
12 canned pear halves and all the
 juice

HOW TO: In a saucepan combine all the above ingredients except the pear halves and bring to a boil. Add the pear halves. Simmer for 15 minutes. Let cool in a bowl; when room temperature, place in the refrigerator. Chill for several hours. Serve in a compote bowl or in individual dishes.

ALMOND SQUARES

These shortbreads are rich and handsome. They are made in a flat pan all at one time, which is a great clean-up feature, and take just ½ hour to bake. If you don't gobble them all up yourself, they can be kept in a jar for two weeks. When neatly arranged, they add elegance to a buffet table. Makes 70 squares.

2 cups flour
¾ cup sugar
1 teaspoon powdered cinnamon
Pinch of salt
½ pound (2 sticks) sweet butter,
 softened

1 egg yolk, lightly beaten
1 egg white, lightly beaten
1 cup slivered or sliced almonds
1 cookie pan (15½" x 10½" x 1")

HOW TO: Preheat oven to 325° F. Sift together the flour, sugar, cinnamon, and salt. Blend in the butter. Work the dough with your hands. Add the lightly beaten egg yolk, and blend well. Dough will be slightly sticky. Spread the dough flat on the pan, patting down gently till about ⅛ inch thick. Don't get discouraged if you think you have too small an amount. Use the palm of your hand to spread the dough, entirely covering the bottom. Moisten fingertips with a little water to ease the process. Brush lightly with beaten egg white. This will also help to smooth the top. Sprinkle almond slices over top and press down lightly into the dough with palm of hand. Bake for ½ hour. Remove from the oven. Let stand 2 to 3 minutes to cool. With sharp knife cut into 1-inch squares, making 9 vertical and 6 horizontal cuts.

3

Be A Passionate C^rook

SPARKLE PLENTY

Here's a baker's dozen for your perusal,
Well insured against a single refusal.
Tripe will make a fantastic meal,
Chaudfroid Vegetables can add a great deal.

Crown Roast of Lamb lets you sparkle plenty,
With Veal Superba you can feed ten or twenty.
For dessert you can flirt with a Topless Tart
Or bake Almond Roll for the beauty part.

OEUFS EN GELÉE

This is an elegant French way to serve an individual portion of an hard-boiled egg with ham. It also adds a decorative touch to the table. Ideal as a summer luncheon dish, it's an appetizer, a jellied soup, and a salad all in one. Prepare it a day in advance and keep in the refrigerator—but do not freeze. This comes via Adele Felheim, a Palm Beach hostess with impeccable taste. Serves 6, can be doubled.

3 large eggs
1 tablespoon gelatin in ¼ cup
  cold water
2 cups clear canned beef
  consommé

2 tablespoons dry sherry or
  port wine
Few sprigs fresh tarragon or
  parsley or dill
6 thin slices boiled ham
1 bunch watercress

HOW TO: Boil the eggs for 6 minutes until hard. Cool and crack under cold running water. Remove the shells carefully and set the eggs aside. Soak the gelatin in ¼ cup of cold water to soften. Heat the beef consommé and then add the softened gelatin. Stir until the gelatin is clear and completely dissolved. Add the sherry or port wine, and cool.

Cut the eggs in half crosswise. Use a lightly oiled custard cup or ramekin for each half egg. Spoon a little of the cooled consommé mixture into the bottom of each mold, about ¼ inch deep. Place in the refrigerator to chill until almost firm. Then set a few sprigs of tarragon or parsley or dill on top of the gelatin and gently place the egg half, *yolk side down*. Spoon more gelatin mixture over the top until egg is almost covered. Cut a circle of the boiled ham to fit the top and set in place on top. Cover with additional gelatin mixture and chill until firm.

When ready to serve, unmold (do not use hot water, just circle with a knife around the inside rim) onto individual salad plates trimmed with watercress. Serve nude—no dressing necessary.

SEAFOOD WITH CHEDDAR AU GRATIN

Le gratin *in France, literally, means "upper crust" (of society); the more familiar* au gratin *means "topped with bread crumbs." The upwardly mobile can reach the top with this elegant dish, which owes its appearance here to Claire Sarnoff of Hollywood, Florida. Its savory, delicate sauce never fails to please guests.*

The secret kick is the stronger flavors of garlic and Worcestershire added to the rich, bland ingredients. The preparation is effortless, and no matter how you serve it, whether in individual scallop shells as an appetizer or surrounded by perfect white rice (see recipe on page 93) as a main course, you will make a dazzling splash as a hostess. Melba toast or toast points are a nice complement. Easily kept warm for drinking guests. Serves 8 to 10.

1 **pound fresh lump crabmeat (frozen may be substituted, but not the canned)**	2 **heaping tablespoons flour**
	1 **cup milk**
½ **pound medium-sized shrimps, shelled and deveined**	½ **cup ketchup**
	½ **pint heavy cream**
½ **pound bay scallops, prepared by boiling in 3 tablespoons white wine**	½ **teaspon garlic salt**
	3 **teaspoons Worcestershire sauce**
	½ **cup grated Cheddar cheese**
¼ **pound (1 stick) butter**	¼ **cup fine bread crumbs**
	Dash of paprika

HOW TO: Preheat oven to 300° F. Pick the crabmeat clean, removing any bits of shell. In a saucepan over low heat make a roux by melting the butter and flour, and then add the milk, stirring constantly to smooth lumps. Remove from heat. Add the ketchup. Fold in the cream, and if too thick, add a little milk. Add the crabmeat, shrimps, and scallops. Flavor with garlic salt, Worcestershire sauce, and Cheddar cheese. When ready to serve, sprinkle with bread crumbs and paprika. Heat for 10 minutes in the oven.

SUGGESTED WINE: BIANCO DELLA COSTA TOSCANA (DRY WHITE IN THE FISH-SHAPED BOTTLE)

TRIPE—THE LIGHT FANTASTIC MEAL!

During a shopping foray at the opening of a new supermarket near our country home, I scanned the neatly piled offerings in the meat department with the hope that my eye would detect an exciting prospect for dinner. I spied some calves' brains—a rarity in most markets. Ah! They might be a bit messy to handle, but remembrances of this delicacy *au beurre noir* eaten in France kept me toying with the possibility. Then I recalled that my husband did not share my enthusiasm for its soft texture. Perhaps some *ris de veau* I mused, as if a French menu were floating before me. I addressed a young girl in a crisp green uniform nearby, who was busy piling more meat packages into the case.

"Are there any sweetbreads available today?"

"Sure," she answered, "just ask in the bakery department—two aisles back there."

I poked around further for sweetbreads, but found none. I did, however, notice a flat package of some leathery, white, honeycombed stuff I had never seen before. It was labeled "tripe." I was aware of tripe, especially the famous French recipe, *Tripe à la Mode de Caen*, a favorite dish for Europeans of both plebian and patrician tastes. In spite of an immediate dislike of its appearance, I decided to find out for myself what the fuss was all about. Can 50 million Frenchmen be wrong? Besides, it was so inexpensive—something I shouldn't pass up. Into the shopping cart it went.

At home I riffled through *The Gold Cook Book* by Louis P. De Gouy, an authoritative French chef. De Gouy's book includes many stories, and is full of interesting information for those who like to read about food as well as cook it. He relates a tale about tripe, in the American Revolution, which is worth reprinting during this Bicentennial year's celebration of our country's founding:

Winter, and General Washington's soldiers were in rags, shoes had worn thin; misery came unrelentingly; food was ever lacking. Cooks made ends meet where were nothing but ends, and they met just over the starvation line. Soldiers began to think of home. Why stay to starve and die at Valley Forge? Desertions were frequent. The story is that General Washington took matters into his own hands and called for the head chef of all the Revolutionary armed forces. He explained the seriousness of the hour. He demanded a great dish. The Chef protested: "There is nothing, my General, but the scraps in the kitchens. There is only tripe—a few hundred pounds, the gift of a nearby butcher. And there are peppercorns, a gift from a Germantown patriot. All the rest is scraps and more scraps."

". . . From nothing," said General Washington, "you must create a great dish." The chef experimented. The tripe was scrubbed, it was simmered tender. Additions went into the big kettles, all the odds and ends of the kitchens. The peppercorns were ground to add fire to the stew. The early darkness came. Great kettles sent up their heart-warming, belly-comforting fragrance to the miserable men. The call of the bugle, and men ate their fill of this fortifying dish. Men laughed again...and they joked: "...Bring on the Red Coats!"

The general called for the chef: "...This dish is the stuff of heroes! What is its name?" "General, I have conceived it but not called it," the chef replied, "But pepper pot would be my humble suggestion, sir." "Call it Philadelphia Pepper Pot," said Washington, "in honor of your home town."

"Pepper Pot . . . Pepper-y Pot, piping hot!" In early days of the Republic the pepper-pot vendor plodded Philadelphia's narrow streets and alleyways chanting the pepper-pot call:

> *"...All hot! All hot!*
> *Pepper pot! Pepper pot!*
> *Make back strong*
> *Makes life long*
> *All hot! Pepper Pot!"*

TRIPE À LA MODE DE NOBLETREES

Here is my version, named for our country place, where we enjoy the fragrant odors while it cooks on winter weekends. Serves 4.

3 pounds fresh honeycomb tripe
3 tablespoons olive oil
2 cloves garlic, sliced
2 yellow onions, finely chopped
1 green pepper, cored and chopped
1 can (12 ounces) whole peeled
  tomatoes

Salt and pepper
 2 bay leaves
 3 sprigs celery leaves
½ teaspoon dried thyme
Jigger of a good red wine or sherry
(optional)

HOW TO: Wash the tripe in 1 or 2 changes of cold water. Put into a 4-quart kettle, cover with cold water, and bring to a boil. Cook for 2 hours until the tripe is tender. Discard the water and put the tripe on a wooden board and cut into very narrow strips (3"x 1").

Into a Dutch oven put the olive oil and garlic. Cook the garlic until light brown; remove with slotted spoon and discard. Then add the onions and green pepper, and cook until onions turn golden. Put in the tomatoes, salt, pepper, bay leaves, celery leaves, and thyme. Add the tripe and cook slowly for about 1 hour over low heat until all the ingredients blend together and the sauce has been reduced to half of the original quantity, and is rich but not too thick or dry. Add the red wine or sherry a few minutes before serving.

The secret of a good tripe is the slow, long cooking, so keep an eye on the pot and add a little water occasionally if you think the sauce is evaporating too quickly.

SUGGESTED WINE: RED RIOJA (HEARTY SPANISH) OR CHELOIS (RED NEW YORK VARIETAL)

BAKED SPINACH À LA GRECQUE

This is a beautiful import with the Greek touch. You may find it served between layers of phyllo dough, the strudel-like pastry used in Greek cooking. It's just as tasty in this simpler version, and year round it will enhance any meal. Baked in a shallow oven-to-table dish (8" x 10"), it offers a new look in green vegetables. Serves 6 to 8.

3 packages frozen chopped spinach	Pinch of salt
¾ cup parsley, finely chopped	¼ teaspoon black pepper
3 scallions, finely chopped	⅛ teaspoon powdered cinnamon
¾ cup fresh dill, finely chopped	4 tablespoons butter
½ pound Feta cheese or pot-style cottage cheese	½ cup sesame seeds

HOW TO: Preheat oven to 375° F. Cook the spinach in boiling salted water and drain thoroughly. Add all the other ingredients except sesame seeds and mix with a fork. Brush a baking dish with melted butter. Spread the spinach mixture in the dish and dot generously with butter. Bake for 30 minutes. Sprinkle with sesame seeds and run under broiler for 3 to 5 minutes to brown seeds. When slightly cooled, cut into squares.

Note: This filling may be used in two 9-inch ready-frozen pastry shells and baked 15 minutes longer until crust is brown.

STUFFED VEGETABLES CHAUDFROID

*This looks like a floral bouquet that's "good enough to eat."
When patty pan squash, deep green spinach, firm red tomatoes,
and large tasty mushrooms appear on the country produce
stands you can assemble this array with ease. Cook the vegetables in the cool morning hours and serve them cold or gently
warmed as the weather or other menu items dictate. Guests
seem to relish this palate pleaser whenever I dish it up. It's a
Hendrix original which you can vary according to your own
seasoning taste. (See color photograph on page 78.) Serves 6
with a portion of each vegetable.*

1 package (10 ounces) frozen chopped spinach or	1 cup prepared seasoned bread crumbs
1 pound fresh spinach, cooked and chopped	¼ cup olive oil
6 small white scalloped summer or patty pan squash	2 or 3 cloves garlic, crushed
6 firm medium-sized tomatoes	2 tablespoons Parmesan cheese, grated
6 large mushrooms	1 tablespoon fresh dill, chopped
1 small yellow onion, finely chopped	1 teaspoon fresh oregano,
	Salt and pepper to taste
	Few parsley sprigs

HOW TO: Prepare the chopped spinach according to the package directions or cook the fresh spinach until tender. Drain and set aside. Clean the squash with cold water, core centers and set aside in a separate dish. Core the whole tomatoes. Fill a saucepan with 2 inches of water and set a small collapsible steamer in it. Place the squash and tomatoes in the pan, cored sides down. Cover and allow to steam, about 15 minutes, over low heat or until vegetables are just fork tender. They should not lose their shape. Remove. Peel the tomatoes (leave skin on squash). Set both vegetables aside.

Gently wash the mushrooms with cold water, remove and chop stems. Arrange mushroom caps, top side up, on a small pie tin coated with a table-spoon of olive oil and place in a 300° F. oven for about 10 minutes, or until they turn brown but still remain firm. Set aside with the tomatoes and squash.

In a small skillet brown half of the chopped onion and the chopped mush-room stems in 1 tablespoon of olive oil. Sauté until the onions are wilted and golden. Add another tablespoon of olive oil, the bread crumbs, oregano, and half of the crushed garlic. Sauté for an additional 2 to 3 minutes, or until the bread crumbs are a medium brown. Add a little olive oil if the mixture seems too dry. The stuffing will be used to fill the mushrooms and should hold together well.

With a spoon generously fill the center of the mushroom caps with the stuffing. Sprinkle stuffed mushroom caps with the Parmesan cheese.

Add the dill to the cooked spinach, season with salt and pepper and a tablespoon of butter, and fill the cored squash with the spinach.

In a skillet sauté the remaining crushed garlic in 1 tablespoon of olive oil. Remove the garlic from the olive oil with a slotted spoon. Add the re-maining chopped onion and squash cores to the garlic-flavored oil and sauté slowly until they are soft enough to mash with a fork. Fill the tomato cen-ters with the squash-onion mixture. Top filled tomatoes with small sprigs of parsley. Arrange all the vegetables on a serving platter and keep at room temperature or store in the refrigerator until ready to serve.

SUGGESTED WINE: RED BORDEAUX (FRENCH CLARET) OR CABERNET SAUVIGNON (CALIFORNIA)

CROWN ROAST OF LAMB ROBERTA

My idea of really fine fixings is a crown roast of lamb. It is one of the special achievements of Roberta Peters, the world famous soprano and a Scarsdale resident. It's a spectacular "casserole" to serve on a platter because the lamb cut in this manner provides a place in which to heap onions, carrots, and Brussels sprouts. Around the roast, the serving platter may be garnished with browned potato balls and mushroom caps filled with peas.

It's a grandiose production that needs the help of your butcher. Ask him to prepare the rack of lamb for a crown roast —and half the work is already done. Be sure that he also provides enough paper frills for each exposed rib-end lamb chop if you want to dress it formally. Serves 8, with 2 ribs per serving.

1 rack of rib lamb chops	**1 package frozen Brussels sprouts**
(approximately 8 pounds)	**12 small potatoes**
Salt and pepper to taste	**1 package frozen baby peas**
2 tablespoons olive oil	**12 large fresh mushrooms**
12 small fresh white onions	**¼ teaspoon dried rosemary**
12 fresh whole baby carrots	

HOW TO: Preheat oven to 375°F. Season the meat with salt and pepper. Brush lightly with olive oil. Wrap aluminum foil around the rib ends to keep them from burning during the cooking process. Place the roast in a roasting pan. Allow 15 minutes per pound cooking time.

Each vegetable should be prepared separately. Glaze the carrots and onions by steaming to fork tenderness and adding a little sugar and butter. Follow package directions for the frozen Brussels sprouts and peas; to the latter, add a little dried rosemary and season with salt and pepper to your taste. The potatoes can be roasted around the meat. The mushroom caps can be prepared by removing the stems and brushing lightly with olive oil and then heating in a separate dish for 10 minutes while meat is roasting. Fill caps with peas and keep warm until ready to trim serving platter.

When the roast is done, remove foil. Fill the center of the roast with glazed onions, baby carrots, and Brussels sprouts. Top each chop bone with a paper frill. Garnish platter with roasted potatoes and mushroom caps filled with peas.

SUGGESTED WINE: CÔTES DE BEAUNE VILLAGES (RED BURGUNDY)

ROAST DUCK WITH CURRANT JELLY GLAZE

To the passionate cuisinière, a tasty roast duckling is a sublime achievement, and worth the work. Nathalie Finkelstein, a Scarsdale friend, serves hers with an unusual glaze that is a welcome change from oranges or cherries.

A word of caution for those climbing these heights for the first time: 1 duckling is adequate for 3 small eaters or 2 hearty ones; so prepare 2 ducklings at one time if serving 4 to 6 people.

4-to-5-pound duckling
Salt and pepper to taste
Sprig of parsley
Sprig of fresh rosemary or
½ teaspoon dried

1 whole onion or whole apple,
  peeled
1 jar (10 ounces) currant jelly

HOW TO: Preheat oven to 400° F. If the bird is frozen, defrost it overnight. Remove the package of giblets from the cavity. Dry the cavity well and cut away any excess fat near the tail. Season the duckling inside and out with salt and pepper. Insert the parsley, rosemary, and onion or apple, as preferred, in the cavity. Place the bird on a rack in an open, shallow roasting pan. After 15 minutes of roasting, prick the flesh at ½-inch intervals all around the legs, thighs, and breast. This allows the fat to escape more easily. Then turn the bird breast side down. Add enough water to fill the pan to about ½ inch to prevent the fat from splattering as it runs off. Roast the bird for 1 hour, removing the pan from the oven once or twice to drain off the accumulated fat and to add fresh water, each time turning the bird to the other side. Remove the duck from time to time with a long fork and let the juices drain from the cavity into a saucepan for easy disposal. When no pink liquid comes out of the cavity when lifted with a fork, and the juices run clear, the duck is ready. Continue to roast, breast side up, until the duckling becomes brown. If you like it very crisp, a 4-pound duckling should roast for about 1½ hours.

Cut the bird in quarters with poultry shears. Lay it skin side up on a broiler pan. Cover the skin with the currant jelly. Place under the broiler, using moderate heat to melt the glaze, about 15 minutes. Remove to a warmed serving platter. Garnish with parsley. If you want gravy to serve on the side, take some of the fat drippings and strain. Set aside ½ cup of drippings and add about a tablespoon of flour, stirring until smooth. Return to the larger quantity. Reheat and serve.

SUGGESTED WINE: BEAUJOLAIS OR PINOT NOIR

CRUSTY BAKED DUCKLING

Roasting a duck turns off some people because the process usually entails handling a large, hot pan while draining off the excess fat that accumulates in the cooking. This recipe eliminates that obstacle as well as the clean-up mess, yet still provides duck lovers with all the succulence they enjoy.

Thanks to Evan and Judith Jones, authors and New York City residents, for this innovation. Serve it with the red hot pepper jelly (see recipe on page 140). Serves 3 to 4.

1 Long Island duckling (about 5 pounds)
2 teaspoons salt
Freshly ground pepper
1 egg
2 tablespoons milk
½ teaspoon dried summer savory (Spice Islands brand)
2 cups fresh bread crumbs
2 tablespoons flour

HOW TO: Preheat oven to 350° F. Peel the skin from duck except on wings. [This is easier to do when the bird is semi-thawed.] Remove as much fat as possible and reserve. Use a very sharp knife or poultry shears to cut out back bone and neck; put these pieces in a pot with the giblets, about 1 teaspoon of salt, a few turns of the pepper grinder, and water to cover amply. Simmer for a couple hours to make stock for sauce. Remove legs, dividing into drumsticks and second joints; remove wings and divide breasts into

4 pieces, easing meat away from the ribs; add bones to stock pot. Cut skin and fat into small pieces and render over low heat. Beat egg with milk, 1 teaspoon salt, several turns of the pepper grinder and savory. Dip duck pieces into this mixture, then roll in seasoned bread crumbs, and brown in a skillet in 2 or 3 tablespoons duck fat. Transfer to a shallow low casserole in which all pieces can lie flat. Cover and bake for about 1 hour. [Uncover for the last 10 minutes if you like it very brown and crisp.] Stir flour into 2 tablespoons of duck fat in a saucepan and add enough of the stock to make sauce.

SUGGESTED WINE: BEAUJOLAIS OR PINOT NOIR

ROCK CORNISH HENS PERSIAN VERSION

Bunnylike breeding has made Rock Cornish hen a popular addition to the twentieth-century cuisine. These full-breasted little birds provide simple servings and generous portions. The Persian version of this stuffing is the type of mishmash that satisfies a creative cook: sweet and spicy flavors, a variety of textures that add panache to the hens. Serve with a salad of watercress or other tart greens and try the Almond Ambrosia Roll (see recipe on page 49) to complete a memorable meal. A half of a bird is ample for most people, though some men will devour a whole bird given the chance. So figure your own quantities from this basic recipe. Serves 3 to 4.

**2 plump Rock Cornish hens
  or small squab chickens**

Stuffing
¼ cup raisins
¼ cup dried currants
12 dried apricot halves, chopped
** 6 whole dried pitted prunes,
   chopped**
** 2 tablespoons celery, chopped**
** 1 apple, peeled and chopped**

**2 tablespoons rendered
  chicken fat or butter**
Salt and pepper to taste

** 1 medium onion, chopped and
   sautéed**
**½ teaspoon fresh thyme or ¼
   teaspoon dried**
**½ teaspoon fresh tarragon or ¼
   teaspoon dried**
¼ teaspoon ground cinnamon

HOW TO: Preheat oven to 350° F. Defrost frozen hens overnight, drain and remove giblets. Rub the chicken fat or butter all over the skin of the birds. Season inside and out with salt and pepper. Blend together all the stuffing ingredients and fill the cavities. Place the birds in an uncovered roasting pan and roast for 1 hour. When done they should be nicely browned all over. Serve or set aside and reheat later if necessary. When reheating, cover the birds with aluminum foil to prevent them from drying out.

SUGGESTED WINE: ORVIETO ABBOCCATO (SEMIDRY ITALIAN) OR NEW YORK SAUTERNE

VEAL SUPERBA FOR ALL SEASONS

Originally called Curried Veal, I gave this entrée more glamorous billing because it's such superlative fare. One of my prized possessions for a formal buffet service, I learned to prepare it at cooking class conducted by Ann Roe Robbins. With her kind permission, I am able to offer below that great discovery. Ingredients and instructions follow hers to the letter, and I advise you to do the same. A bonus for the cook is that it may be made ahead of time and then reheated in a double boiler over simmering water, leaving the host or hostess at ease. Serves 6.

6 cups water	2 pounds cubed leg of veal
3 medium carrots	8 tablespoons butter
7 small white onions	4 tablespoons flour
1 leek	2 teaspoons curry powder
1 stalk celery	2 cups strained veal stock
1 clove garlic	½ cup light cream
1 bay leaf	1 pound mushrooms
2 teaspoons salt	1 tablespoon sugar
4 whole peppercorns	1 tablespoon parsley, finely chopped

47

HOW TO: First make a good veal stock. Place the water in a heavy deep saucepan. Slice one of each of the following and add to the water: a carrot, an onion, a leek, a celery stalk, a clove of garlic. Season with the bay leaf, salt, and peppercorns. Bring to a boil and then add the veal. Bring to a boil again, lower heat, and let simmer for 1 to 1¼ hours or until meat is tender. Remove the meat with a slotted spoon and set aside. Strain off and set aside 2 cups of the stock. To the remaining stock, add the remaining 6 peeled whole onion and the other 2 carrots. Let boil for 20 minutes. Remove and drain the vegetables from stock and set aside.

In the top of a double boiler over direct heat melt 4 tablespoons of butter and add the flour and curry powder. To this flavored roux add the 2 cups of the drained veal stock and stir until the mixture comes to a boil. Remove from heat and add the cream. Add the cooked veal to the sauce. Place the top of the double boiler over simmering water and cook for ½ hour.

To prepare the vegetables, cut the mushrooms in halves or quarters, depending on their size. In a medium-sized skillet sauté mushrooms in 4 tablespoons of butter until lightly browned. Remove the mushrooms from the pan and set aside. Place the cooked onions and carrots in the skillet and sprinkle with a little sugar until they are glazed. Add the vegetables to the veal in the cream sauce.

This may be served when all is hot or kept almost indefinitely over simmering water. It may also be prepared in advance and reheated. It is best served with white rice and chutney or other condiments, as you prefer. Sprinkle with parsley.

SUGGESTED WINE: NEW YORK SAUTERNE (DRY WHITE)

ALMOND AMBROSIA ROLL

When the ancient gods of Greece feasted at Parnassus on nectar and ambrosia, they must have climaxed the event with an aromatic light dessert such as this one.

I experienced its heavenly taste at a buffet party given by Helen M. Palley, an accomplished hostess active in artistic and philanthropic causes in New York City. The scent of cinnamon wafting from her pantry led me toward the kitchen, where I saw a caterer put this marvel together. I swooned.

Frank Paliotta, the chef of the CBS Radio Executives Dining Room in New York, parted with these easy-to-follow directions. When I duplicated the cake at home, I sent it to Lena Horne through a mutual friend, to present to her after a gala performance. This exquisite entertainer, who glows onstage, became equally lyrical offstage over the taste sensation of Almond Ambrosia Roll. Serves 8 greedy people generously.

1 cup toasted blanched almonds (available in 5½-ounce can)	1 cup plus 2 tablespoons sugar
	Vegetable oil
5 eggs, separated	½ cup confectioners' sugar
½ teaspoon salt	1 pint heavy cream for whipping
1 teaspoon cinnamon	1 teaspoon vanilla extract

HOW TO: Preheat oven to 375° F. Grind the almonds coarsely in a blender, about 15 seconds. Do not overdo as they will become too powdered or oily. Mix the cinnamon with 1 cup of sugar.

Line a cookie pan (15½"x 10½"x 1") with waxed paper, waxed side down. With the fingers very lightly oil the top side of the paper and about ½ inch up the sides of the pan.

Beat the egg whites with a pinch of salt until very stiff and peaky. Beat the egg yolks in a separate bowl until creamy and thick. Take half of the cinnamon-sugar mixture and add it to the egg yolks. Then fold in half of the ground almonds. Alternately fold the remaining half of the cinnamon-sugar mixture, the yolk-almond mixture, and the remaining ground almonds into the egg whites. Use a wooden spoon to prevent the egg whites from breaking down.

Pour the mixture evenly on top of the wax paper and bake for 15 minutes, or until the cake pulls away from the edge. Remove from the oven and allow to cool. Place a second piece of wax paper on top and turn the cake over, allowing it to rest on the fresh paper. After you remove old paper spread the top of the cake with half of the whipped cream to which vanilla extract has been added. Roll up the cake on the long side by picking up one end of the fresh wax paper and, using fingers to turn cake edge under, begin to roll cake. Sprinkle the top of the roll with powdered confectioners' sugar. Cut into triangular slices about 1 inch thick or for larger portions into rolls about 2 inches wide. Top each slice with a dollop of whipped cream.

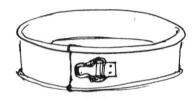

VIENNESE APPLE KUCHEN

This authentic Viennese dessert is a dressy version of an apple dish made with a cookie dough base. Its obvious home-baked appearance makes it worth your special effort.

Laura Odell of New York City, a friend whose culinary talents led her to a successful career as a designer of kitchens, graciously prepared this in mine. I followed her instructions when I made it alone and found that it tested triple A-1.

Use an 8-inch spring-form pan and allow to cool 2 to 3 hours before serving. Top with whipped cream for added glamour. (See color photograph on page 75.) Serves 8 generously.

¼ **pound (1 stick) sweet butter,
 softened at room temperature**
1 ½ **cups unbleached flour**
1 **teaspoon baking powder**
½ **cup sugar**
1 **egg**
6 or 7 **large McIntosh apples
 (4 heaping cupfuls)**

¼ **cup tightly packed raisins
 or currants**
⅓ **cup dark brown sugar**
1 ½ **teaspoons ground cinnamon**
Confectioners' sugar
½ **pint heavy cream, whipped**
2 **tablespoons sugar**
1 **teaspoon vanilla extract**

50

HOW TO: Preheat oven to 375° F. Generously butter the spring-form pan, bottom and sides. Add sufficient flour to dust all over, discarding any excess. Place pan in the refrigerator until ready to line with dough.

In a bowl blend the butter with the flour and baking powder which have been sifted together, add the sugar, and mix all with your hands until it resembles coarse oatmeal. Drop in the unbeaten egg and continue to blend by hand. It will finally form into a ball.

Set aside ⅓ of a cup of the dough for use later as a topping. Divide the remaining dough into four equal parts.

On a lightly floured board or counter, using a lightly floured rolling pin, roll out one of the dough portions into a circle, approximately 8½ inches in diameter and ⅛ inch thick. Place it in the bottom of the prepared spring-form so that the outer edge of the circle rises about ¼ inch up the sides of the pan.

Roll the remaining three parts of the dough into long narrow strips, ⅛ inch thick. Take the first strip and lay it around the inside of the pan, pressing the bottom edge so that it overlays and seals the edge of the bottom layer of dough and press the strip firmly against the pan sides as if you were working with clay. Do the same with the remaining strips of dough until you have a pan completely and tightly lined with a shell of dough. Set it in the refrigerator while you prepare the apple mixture.

Quarter the apples, then carefully peel them, removing all parts of the core. Cut apple quarters crosswise from the top down in ½-inch-thick pieces, about three per quarter. Mix the raisins or currants, brown sugar, and cinnamon, to make about ½ cup, and add to the apples. If the mix seems tart, adjust the sugar and cinnamon to taste. Place the seasoned apples in the dough-lined pan.

Now comes the trick that makes this a beauty. Take the ⅓ cup of dough reserved and roll it out on a floured surface into a circle 7 inches in diameter, and gently place it on top of the apple mixture, leaving about a 1-inch space around the edge of the pan.

Bake for 45 minutes until the crust is a light brown. Remove the kuchen from the oven and let cool for an hour. You will notice that the inside crust begins to pull away from the pan. You can help the process a bit by running a knife around the outer edge of the kuchen, being careful not to break the crust. Release the spring form. Sift some confectioners' sugar on the top crust.

When ready to serve, whip the cream with the sugar and vanilla extract. Serve in a separate bowl for individual helpings.

PLUM OR PEACH TOPLESS TART

Here's an eye-catching topless tart that men can shamelessly enjoy. It makes an elegant addition for buffet service, especially during the late summer when fresh fruits are in season. As one's kitchen can be a hot spot at that time of year, I make it in the cool of the morning. No need to roll out dough—you pat this dough into the pan. This is a special accomplishment of Helen Shockley of White Plains, New York. Note: When making the plum version, use only the dark-purple, freestone variety. (See color photograph on page 79.) Serves 10.

1½ cups flour
¾ cup sugar
1 teaspoon baking powder
Pinch of salt
¼ pound (1 stick) butter, cut in half

1 egg, slightly beaten
¼ cup milk (optional)
2½ pounds peaches or plums, pitted
¼ cup sugar to sprinkle over fruit
1 jar (10 ounces) currant jelly to glaze

HOW TO: Preheat oven to 375° F. Sift the flour, sugar, baking powder, and salt into a bowl. Add ½ stick of the butter and the egg. Knead all together until the batter is pliable, but not too sticky. If it is too dry, add a little milk. Flatten the dough on a lightly greased and lightly floured oblong pan (15½"x 10½"x 1"). Dough can be spread more easily when the fingers are slightly moistened with water. For plums, cut in half, and place about ½ inch apart in rows, skin side down. Press them slightly into dough. In the center of each half, sprinkle sugar, and, using the other ½ stick of butter, put little dots of butter in each.

For peaches, peel and cut into wedge shapes (not too thin), and lay aside in straight rows until pan is completely covered. Press them slightly into the dough, and sprinkle with sugar and dots of butter as above. Bake for 30 minutes. When the tart is cooled, glaze it by gently spooning melted, slightly cooled currant jelly over the entire tart. This gives it a very professional look. Tastes better too.

4

Be An Oriental Faker

FIX EASTERN FARE WITH A FLAIR

Try ten in this chapter, authentic and rare
Ways to fix Far Eastern fare with a flair.
Wing Dings or Spareribs are fine for a start,
Fry Beef or Chicken for a meal à la carte.

Learn to toss vegetables in the Japanese fashion,
Javanese Rice could become your great passion.
Arrange delicate fruits like mandarin's mammy,
Or blend them in Ambrosia with a Double Whammy.

CHICKEN WING DINGS

A dieter's delight, this chicken hors d'oeuvre needs no bread, crackers, or even toothpicks—just your fingertips to bring it from the serving dish to your lips. It's a neat trick from those clever Chinese who serve it in Hong Kong.

Chicken wings are easy to fix. Like other chicken parts, wings come packaged in quantities in the poultry section of the supermarket. Wing Dings may be frozen and kept for several weeks, then thawed and warmed to treat unexpected guests to a fine homemade dish. Serve with sweet duck-sauce dip or just plain. When cold, the flavors are very subtle, and the ingredients remain a mystery. Serves 12.

16 chicken wings	**1 cup water**
2 tablespoons vegetable oil	**½ cup dry sherry**
2 scallions, coarsely chopped	**1 clove garlic, crushed**
½ cup soy sauce	**2 slices ginger root, minced**

HOW TO: Remove the last joint (tip) from the chicken wings. (I freeze tips and add them to chicken soup at some future time.) In a skillet heat the oil and brown the chicken wings quickly. Add all the remaining ingredients. Bring to a boil. Cover and simmer gently for ½ hour. Let stand to cool. Remove chicken wings from the sauce. Cut into 2 parts for easy finger service. Serve warm or cold, as desired.

SPICY SPARERIBS

Ruby Marzan, my invaluable aide-de-cuisine who comes from Alabama, finds Chinese food very much to her family's taste. This succulent, crisp way to dip into an Oriental meal is her original recipe, with a Southern touch. It has a good zesty flavor which can be adjusted to your own liking. Some people prefer to leave the spareribs whole, but it's more convenient to handle them gracefully in smaller portions. Serve with hot Chinese mustard and sweet duck sauce. Serves 4 to 6.

4 pounds pork spareribs, separated,
  with each rib chopped into 3-inch
  pieces
1 cup ketchup
1 teaspoon prepared mustard
4 teaspoons soy sauce

2 cloves garlic, crushed
2 tablespoons dry sherry or wine
  vinegar
1 teaspoon paprika
1 cup water

HOW TO: Preheat oven to 400° F. Place the spareribs in a flat roasting pan. Mix all the other ingredients into a sauce and pour over the ribs. Roast, uncovered, in the oven for 1 hour at 400° F., then lower heat to 350° F. for another 40 minutes to 1 hour. Baste 3 or 4 times during the roasting process and coat the meat well. Here is the trick of this recipe: To be sure that the spareribs don't burn, but still stay crisp, add a little water to the pan if the sauce becomes too thick.

SUGGESTED WINE: SAKE (JAPANESE RICE WINE) OR GAMAY NOIR (RED CALIFORNIA)

CHINESE CHICKEN WITH VEGETABLES

The secret of Chinese "Quick Cook Dinners" is to prepare the main ingredients early in the morning and keep them crisp in the refrigerator. When you come home at the day's end, dog-tired and hungry, it's literally a matter of minutes—about 10 to be exact—till dinner.

Wash and cut all the vegetables into slivers, and refrigerate in plastic bags. This also applies to the chicken breasts, which can marinate in a dish until ready for use. Weight watchers please note: This recipe uses no corn starch. Be sure to have all the ingredients assembled before you start. Serves 4.

2 tablespoons soy sauce
2 tablespoons dry sherry
½ cup chicken broth
2 chicken breasts, skinned, bonded,
  cut into strips (2″x ½″)
¼ cup peanut oil
3 cups bok choy (Chinese cabbage),
  cut into slivers

¼ pound fresh snow pea pods or
  1 package frozen
1 cup water chestnuts, sliced
1 cup fresh bean sprouts
¼ pound fresh mushrooms, sliced
¼ cup toasted almond slivers
  (available in 5½-ounce can)

HOW TO: Prepare a marinade of the soy sauce, sherry, and 2 tablespoons of the chicken broth. Pour over the strips of chicken breasts and let stand in the refrigerator at least 1 hour or longer until you are ready to cook and serve the dish.

Drain the chicken and reserve the marinade. Heat a teflon-lined skillet or a wok and add 1 tablespoon of the oil to coat the pan. Over high heat toss in the chicken and stir fry quickly (2 to 3 minutes) until the meat turns white, but is still tender. Add the marinade and cook for few seconds. Remove the chicken and the sauce from the pan and set it aside in a dish in a warm place.

Wipe the pan or wok to reuse it to cook the prepared sliced vegetables. Add a tablespoon of the oil to the pan and over high heat, for 2 minutes, toss in the bok choy, or Chinese cabbage, the snow pea pods, and cook for 60 seconds using a wooden chopstick to stir the vegetables constantly. Lower the heat to moderate, then add the remaining soy sauce and chicken broth. Cover and cook for 1 minute more. Add the water chestnuts and mushrooms and cook another 30 seconds, or until all the vegetables are warmed through. Add a little soy sauce to adjust to your taste. Place the vegetables in a warmed deep dish, add the chicken and toss the almonds on top over all. Serve immediately.

SUGGESTED WINE: EST! EST!! EST!!! (WHITE DRY ITALIAN)

SWEET & SOUR SEA BASS

The well-known Chinese cookbook author, Jim Lee, of New York City says, "Sea bass is one of the favorite fish of the Chinese people. As with all fish, sea bass must not be overcooked or else its wonderful qualities will be lost beyond recall." Here are his instructions in the Chinese manner.

Use a sea bass about 1½ to 2 pounds in size. Bigger sea bass can be used, but most home kitchens are not equipped to deep fry such large creatures. It is better to make two smaller fish in such cases, when you have company. Make two or three fairly deep slashes diagonally across the fish's body on both sides before breading and deep frying; this speeds the cooking.

You must adjust the frying time according to the size of the fish. Generally, the fish is done, regardless of size, when the skin with the breading becomes golden brown. Serves 4.

2 carrots, sliced

3 scallions, cut into 1 ½-inch lengths (including green tops)

2 slices canned pineapple, cut into wedges

½ cup vinegar

½ cup sugar

½ cup chicken stock

⅛ teaspoon salt

1 tablespoon cornstarch

1 fresh sea bass, about 1 ½ to 2 pounds, cleaned

Salt and pepper to taste

½ cup flour

Vegetable oil for deep-frying

1 green pepper, sliced

HOW TO: Prepare the sweet and sour sauce first. In a saucepan place the carrots, scallions, pineapple, vinegar, sugar, and chicken stock. Bring to a boil. Lower heat and simmer for 15 minutes. Add the cornstarch, stirring thoroughly until the sauce has thickened. Turn the heat very low, just enough to keep the sauce hot until ready for use.

Dry the fish. Sprinkle with salt and pepper inside and out. Spread ½ cup of flour on a piece of wax paper or aluminum foil. Roll the fish in the flour to cover the skin lightly. In a large deep-frying pan heat the oil to about 375° F. With a pair of tongs, or other long-handled kitchen utensil, gently lower the fish into the oil. Cook for about 5 minutes until the skin turns golden brown. Remove the fish onto absorbent paper to drain off the excess oil.

Turn heat to high under the sweet and sour sauce. Add the green pepper slices. Stir and cook for 1 minute. Place the fish on a serving platter, ladle the sweet and sour sauce over it, and serve at once.

SUGGESTED WINE: LIEBFRAUMILCH HANNS CHRISTOF (GERMAN RHINE)

BEEF WITH VEGETABLES

Here's another one of Jim Lee's infallible Chinese recipes. A treat for an Oriental feast to serve in conjunction with a chicken or fish dish—"one from Column A and one from Column B." Plain white rice (see recipe on page 93) goes well with all Chinese dishes. Be sure to serve plenty of piping hot tea. Serves 4.

1 teaspoon sugar
2 teaspoons cornstarch
2 tablespoons oyster sauce
¼ cup chicken broth or water
1 small can button mushrooms, drained, liquid saved
1 tablespoon vegetable oil
2 cups sirloin steak, trimmed and cut into 1-inch cubes
3 tablespoons light soy sauce

2 tablespoons gin or vodka
2 tablespoons vegetable oil
1 cup diced bok choy hearts or celery cabbage
½ cup bamboo shoots, diced
¼ cup water chestnuts, diced (fresh or canned)
1 cup snow pea pods
¼ cup parsley (optional)
¼ cup nut meats (optional)

HOW TO: For the sauce, mix together the sugar, cornstarch, oyster sauce, chicken broth or water, and liquid from mushrooms, and put aside.

Heat the wok or frying pan hot and dry. Add 1 tablespoon of the oil and heat till very hot. Add the steak cubes. Sear on one side and then turn them over until cubes are brown. Combine the soy sauce and the gin or vodka and pour over the steak; turn heat off immediately. Remove the steak and juice from wok or pan into bowl and put aside.

Wash the wok or pan and reheat till hot and dry. Add the 2 tablespoons of oil. Put in all the fresh and canned vegetables except the snow peas. Stir-fry for 2 minutes. Cover and cook for 1 minute more.

Remove the cover and stir in the sauce mixture until it thickens. Add the snow peas and stir thoroughly. Put back steak and juice, and mix. Remove from pan to serving dish. Top with parsley or chopped nut meats, as desired.

SUGGESTED WINE: VALPOLICELLA (RED VERONESE) OR PINOT NOIR (CALIFORNIA)

GREEN PEPPER, ONIONS, & ZUCCHINI
JAPANESE STYLE

One of the surprises of a visit to Japan is the simplicity of some of its less publicized cuisine.

In Kyoto I was introduced to a well-known home-cooked dish called shabu-shabu, *ordered a day in advance by our guide. We were traveling with a small group of architects and their wives, and this was set before us as we sat in a semicircle around a low table where we could view the graceful young waitresses, with the deft touch of a juggler, cook our meal in a steaming kettle of broth. Large trays of pre-sliced thin circlets of vegetables and wafer-thin portions of beef were maneuvered with chopsticks in the kettle. Each immersion took a few seconds to cook. It was a fascinating performance.*

This is my simplified version of that unique eating experience. I use green pepper, sweet Bermuda onion, and zucchini for mine; but you may substitute or add white turnips, broccoli, or string beans, as you prefer.

The delicate, bland flavor of Japanese cooking sneaks up on you in a most satisfying way. Slicing the vegetables in circles rather than slivers is one characteristic that distinguishes Japanese cuisine from other Oriental fare. Quick, stir-fry methods are identical with those used by the Chinese. Serves 4.

1 tablespoon sesame or peanut oil
1 clove garlic, cut into 3 slivers
1 large Bermuda onion, peeled and cut into thin circles (⅛ inch)
2 green peppers, cored and cut into thin rings (⅛ inch)
2 medium-sized zucchinis, or 1 large, cleaned, unpeeled, cut into thin circles (⅛ inch) or other assorted vegetables as you prefer prepared the same way
1 tablespoon soy sauce
1 cup beef or chicken broth made with bouillon cube

HOW TO: Lightly coat a teflon pan or a wok with sesame seed or peanut oil. Add the garlic and remove with a slotted spoon when it turns light brown. Toss in the onions, stir-fry for 1 to 2 minutes. Add the green peppers, stir-fry for another 2 minutes, then toss in the zucchini. Add the soy sauce and chicken broth; stir the vegetables well and cook, covered, for about 2 to 3 minutes. With a bowl of noodles this is a wonderful meatless meal. Try Fruits Mandarin (see recipe on page 61) for dessert.

JAVANESE RICE

You can almost make a main dish out of Javanese Rice. It's wonderful buffet fare for both Western and Eastern menus, and is one of the few Oriental-style foods that does not use soy sauce.

It was first introduced to me by my sister, Elga Duval, a talented artist and adventurous cook who lives in Huntington, Long Island. This dish may be assembled several hours in advance and given its finishing touches a minute before serving time. Serves 4 to 6.

6 eggs	1 cup raw rice
4 scallions, finely chopped	1 teaspoon lemon juice
(including green tops)	2 tablespoons peanut oil
1 teaspoon salt	

HOW TO: Beat the eggs well. Add the chopped scallions and salt, and let the mixture stand in the refrigerator 2 to 3 hours. Prepare the rice (see recipe on page 93), adding only lemon juice as seasoning. When ready to serve, heat the peanut oil in a heavy iron skillet. Let it get very hot. Add the egg mixture for 1 minute, add the cooked rice, turn off heat and stir gently as eggs cover rice. Place in a warm serving dish.

OPEN SESAME STRING BEANS

Here's a shortcut that gives Eastern flavor to that very un-exotic vegetable—string beans. Consider this little number next time you need a cool salad. Or try string beans hot, dressed with sesame seeds instead of almonds or mushrooms. Serves 4 to 6.

**1 pound fresh green string beans
 (remove tips)
4 tablespoons soy sauce**

**2 teaspoons sesame or
 peanut oil
2 teaspoons sesame seeds**

HOW TO: Cook the whole string beans for 5 minutes in boiling water until just blanched. Drain under cold water to make them crisp. Season with soy sauce and sprinkle with oil. Place in a salad bowl or warmed vegetable dish and add sesame seeds.

FRESH FRUITS MANDARIN

For a grand Oriental flourish, a dessert to set before the Princess Turandot, this is a beautiful spectacle. I have added the liqueur for a bit of East-meets-West. Fortune cookie say, "You will travel to enchanted country." Serves 6 to 8.

**¾ cup lemon-flavored marmalade
1 tablespoon lemon juice
2 tablespoons orange juice
2 grapefruits, peeled, sectioned,
 seeded
3 navel oranges, peeled,
 sectioned, seeded**

**2 bananas, peeled and sliced at
 an angle
2 tablespoons orange Curaçao or
 Cointreau (optional)
1 small can (6 ounces) fresh water-
 packed lichee nuts
2 tablespoons crystallized ginger,
 chopped**

HOW TO: In a small heavy saucepan melt the marmalade over low heat, stirring occasionally. Remove from the heat and add the lemon and orange juices. Let cool. Place the grapefruit and orange sections in a shallow serving bowl. Stir in the cooled marmalade mixture. Place in the refrigerator to chill. Just before serving, slice bananas and add them to the bowl, mixing gently. Pour in the liqueur and garnish with lichee nuts and ginger.

DOUBLE WHAMMY AMBROSIA

As a variation on kumquats or the almond or fortune cookies that are the usual dessert finale to an Oriental meal, here's an ideal combination. It can be made a day or, even better, two days ahead of time, and refrigerated until ready to serve. Since there is no cooking involved, only refrigeration, it's excellent summer fare.

Once you've tried Ambrosia this way, you'll probably agree with me that its fruity, rich flavor pairs well with most any dish. It's a beautifully concocted dessert as befits the lady from whom I received it—Ida Webster, a busy New York architect who manages to entertain frequently with grace and taste. Serves 8.

1 can (20 ounces) pineapple chunks
2 cans (10 ounces each) mandarin
   oranges
1 pint heavy sour cream

½ package (2 cups)
   mini-marshmallows
1 jigger Grand Marnier
½ cup sweetened shredded
   coconut

HOW TO: Drain the canned fruits thoroughly. You can save juices for a future fruit drink. Place the fruits in a bowl and add the sour cream, mini-marshmallows, and Grand Marnier. Mix thoroughly. Keep in the refrigerator at least 24 hours—or, better still, 48 hours—stirring once or twice to be sure all ingredients are well blended. The whole mixture marries into a firm, creamy affair. When ready to serve, sprinkle generously with shredded coconut.

5

Dig For Buried Treasure

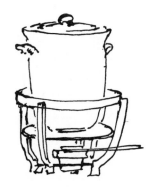

FIND FAMILY JEWELS

Some homemade dishes may seem rather trite
But to many they are an ethnic delight.
Keep your eye on those who cook with rules,
It's the best place to find family jewels.

Two noodle favorites are herein revealed,
Their secret proportions have long been concealed.
Try Sybil's Bouillabaise—it's the best ever made.
To dig Momshie's Cookies you don't need a spade.

MATZO BALLS—AN ACT OF FAITH?

To some people certain dishes are part of their religion. My father used to say that in our faith there were three sects—Orthodox, Reform, and Gastronomic. Matzo balls are a traditional part of the Passover seder, but for some fervent Gastronomic adherents, they are frequently served at a Friday night pre-Sabbath dinner. On the other hand, for those who do not regard matzo balls as part of their devotions, there's such a thing as TOO MUCH.

Abie's Irish Rose was heard to tentatively suggest to her mother-in-law after several months of the monotonous Friday night menu, "Mama, the matzo balls are delicious—but couldn't you make something and use a different part of the matzo for a change?"

A favorite story about how one matzo ball recipe was tossed around is no doubt apocryphal, but it illustrates the circuitous route a recipe can often travel. When Marilyn Monroe married Arthur Miller, she was no less eager than any other bride to prepare her husband's favorite dishes. He expressed a great preference for matzo balls, a dish which she had never even heard about. Not wanting to betray her ignorance, she telephoned Elizabeth Taylor, who was then the experienced Jewish wife of movie mogul Mike Todd. Marilyn (in Connecticut) hoped that Liz (in Hollywood) would have the recipe for making matzo balls. Elizabeth reassured her: "Of course, I have. Mike loves the way I make them, and I am sure Arthur will, too." Then like neighborly housewives anywhere, Elizabeth told, while Marilyn took notes—long distance.

Recipe in hand, Marilyn produced the matzo balls, floating in a bowl of chicken soup. They delighted Arthur, "Marvelous—as good as my mother's any day." In gratitude, Marilyn called Elizabeth again to describe the joy of her first successful cooking venture. With lavish praise she thanked her for her help. "They were wonderful and seasoned just the way Arthur likes them. Where did you ever get the recipe?" Elizabeth blithely explained: "Oh, that was easy—from Sammy Davis, Jr."

Among matzo ball cognoscenti they are frequently called "sinkers" or "floaters." Whichever type you prefer, be sure to serve 3 per person in a clear, fat-free chicken broth, with a bit of chopped parsley scattered on top to set off this jewel.

MATZO BALLS—FLOATERS

Most family treasures include at least one of "mother's traditional recipes." Nathalie Finkelstein's mother bequeathed her this prize, and she, in turn, shares it with her children and grandchildren. I have tasted all varieties and sizes of matzo balls, but none better than this — even my Japanese friends adore it. To all readers I simply say, "Try it, you'll like it!"

Plan to make the matzo meal mix at least 3 hours ahead of time so that it will have a chance to cool in the refrigerator before you start to form the balls. A mere 20 minutes to cook, and Presto—Soupo! The balls are ready for the chicken soup, their traditional companion. (See recipe on page 66.)

Matzo balls are also frequently served as dumplings with chicken or meat; then they should be heated in the oven with a little extra coating of chicken fat to help brown them. Yields 24 matzo balls.

4 eggs	1 teaspoon nutmeg
⅓ cup cold water	(my addition)
2 teaspoons salt	6 tablespoons melted chicken fat
¼ teaspoon pepper	1¼ cups matzo meal
	2 quarts water, lightly salted

HOW TO: Beat the eggs. Add the cold water, salt, pepper, nutmeg, and melted chicken fat. Blend well. Then stir in the matzo meal. Mixture should be stiff, but not too solid. Place in the refrigerator for at least 3 hours or leave overnight.

In a large deep saucepan bring the 2 quarts of lightly salted water to a rapid boil. Remove the matzo meal mixture from the refrigerator and form into balls about 1¼ inches round. Gently put the matzo balls into the boiling water and boil slowly for 20 minutes, until fluffy and tender. Remove, drain, and set aside in refrigerator till needed. About 15 minutes before serving, add the matzo balls to a clear chicken soup (see recipe on page 66) and simmer. Do not boil or leave them in the soup too long—they absorb the liquid, and you will be left with very little soup.

MARROW MATZO BALLS

Here's a recipe with obvious German roots, marrow being a frequently used ingredient in German cooking. This is a specialty of Helen Treeger, a multitalented homemaker of New York City.

Her version of matzo balls can be assembled long in advance, frozen, and kept indefinitely until a holiday occasion arises. Rolled into 1-inch rounds, the ingredients below will make almost 40 small matzo balls. They give a big dinner a light start. Serves 12.

2 beef marrow bones, about 2½ inches across	**½ teaspoon paprika**
2 tablespoons softened butter	**1 tablespoon parsley, minced**
½ teaspoon salt	**3 eggs, well beaten**
	¾ cup matzo meal

HOW TO: Scoop out the beef marrow from the uncooked beef bones. You should have about ⅓ cup of marrow. Cream it together with the softened butter. Add the salt, paprika, parsley, and eggs, and mix well. Then add the matzo meal, which will make the mixture the consistency of cottage cheese. Let stand 20 minutes, then refrigerate for at least 3 hours or freeze. When ready to use, roll the matzo meal mixture into small balls, about the size of sour-ball candies, 1 inch in diameter. Boil, uncovered, in 2 quarts of salted water for 25 minutes. Drain and add to the chicken soup. Do not boil the matzo balls in the soup.

CLASSY CHICKEN SOUP

Many people have a favorite scratch recipe for chicken soup. Others are quite content with brews made from bouillon cubes or powders or with the canned variety. Matzo balls are compatible with any form of chicken broth, but I prefer the homemade soup and find it no effort to make several quarts at a time, storing what I don't use in the refrigerator. This recipe also has a hidden bonus—the chicken parts provide enough meat for a small salad, too, and you haven't sacrificed a whole chicken. Real economy all the way. Yields 4 quarts; serves 12.

1 pound each of wings, backs, and necks (3 pounds in all)
2 celery stalks with leaves, coarsely chopped
2 yellow onions, coarsely chopped
2 carrots, scraped and cut into ¼-inch slices
1 parsnip, scraped and cut into chunks
1 leek, trimmed of all greens and cut crosswise into 3 pieces
4 parsley sprigs
4 quarts cold water
Salt and pepper to taste

HOW TO: Thoroughly wash and dry the chicken parts and put into a 6-quart kettle. Then place all the vegetables and parsley into the kettle and cover with water. Season with salt and pepper and bring to a boil over high heat. Lower to a simmer and let cook for 1 hour. Remove from the heat and pick out all chicken parts with a slotted spoon. Set aside in a separate dish. Also remove the carrots and set aside separately, to add to the clear soup when finished. Strain the remaining vegetables, reserving as much juice for the soup as possible. Set aside the vegetables. The clear chicken broth may now be seasoned with additional salt and pepper to your taste. Return the carrot slices only after you have poured the soup into quart-sized jars for easy storage in the refrigerator, ready for serving whenever you wish, heated and sprinkled with parsley.

The vegetable pulp can be puréed in a blender with a tablespoon of the liquid and stored in another jar. It can be added to the clear broth if you like it thicker. If you prefer a stronger tasting chicken soup, toss in a chicken bouillon cube. The wings are a nice addition to the soup, one in each serving.

For a salad, discard the skin from the chicken parts, remove the meat and save, chill, and add some diced celery and mayonnaise to make a lovely chicken salad.

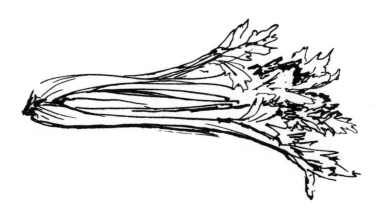

BOUILLABAISSE À LA SYBIL

There is no language adequate to describe the flavor and aroma of this bouillabaisse. The recipe for the famous Provençal fish soup comes from a dear friend, Sybil Hartfield of Los Angeles. She showed me how she makes it during a recent visit to our country home.

Together we purchased each ingredient carefully — every seasoning tossed was measured exactly. But, as I observed along the way, the most valuable ingredients cannot be listed in any recipe: a good right arm for dicing vegetables and a fine sense of taste to test the many flavors added during the cooking process.

Like the rare gem that it is, bouillabaisse deserves a beautiful setting. A lovely, large soup tureen and deep, old-fashioned soup plates are ideal. Serve a tossed green salad, so guests can have something to nibble while the ritual of ladling the bouillabaisse receives its proper attention.

French bread (see recipe on page 116), sliced lengthwise through the middle, spread with garlic butter and toasted under the broiler to a light brown, should accompany the bouillabaisse. Chilled rosé wine plus a very lemony-flavored dessert—the Unforgettable Lemon Torte (see recipe on page 21) is ideal—et voilà . . . perfection. Both these original recipes make their first public appearance in this book.

The sauce for the bouillabaisse may be made a day in advance. Add all of the fish an hour before serving. The final dollop of shellfish is added minutes before eating time. Serves 8 happily.

Sauce

¾ cup olive or vegetable oil
1 green pepper, very finely diced
3 large yellow onions, very finely diced
1 whole bunch celery, very finely diced (stalks and leaves)
2 cloves garlic, minced
2 large cans (2 pounds 3 ounces each) tomatoes
3 bay leaves

2 tablespoons salt
2½ tablespoons sugar
Juice of 1 lemon
8 peppercorns
2 teaspoons seasoned salt
½ teaspoon cayenne pepper
3 teaspoons dried oregano
½ teaspoon dried rosemary
½ teaspoon dried basil
¼ teaspoon chili powder
1 cup medium dry sherry

Fish

1 pound each any firm fish (sea
bass, red snapper, Boston
bluefish, scrod, or halibut,
skinned and boned, for a total
of 3 pounds). Fish should remain
chunky and firm even after an
hour of cooking.

2 cans (6 ounces each) whole
baby clams

1 pound bay or sea scallops

½ pound fresh mushrooms, sliced

1 pound fresh shrimp, shelled
and deveined

1 or 2 small lobsters, uncooked in
shell, cut into chunks

1 or 2 hard-shell crabs, cut into
chunks

HOW TO: Put the olive or vegetable oil in a large 6-quart saucepan and add
the green pepper, onion, celery and garlic. Cook for about 20 minutes over
moderate heat, stirring occasionally, until all the vegetables begin to wilt.
Mash the tomatoes to break down the pulp, so it is like a rich sauce, then
add to the mixture, stirring well. Add the seasonings, herbs, lemon juice
and ½ cup of sherry. Stir contents thoroughly. Taste once or twice to get the
flavor so that you will notice the difference as the cooking progresses.
Simmer, covered, for 1 hour over low heat. This is the point at which the
sauce may be cooled and stored. It will be very thick, but will thin a bit
when the fish is added. Allow 1 hour from reheating to serving time.

Prepare the fish by cutting raw, filleted, boned, and skinned fish into 3-inch
chunks. Reheat the sauce and add the fish to the hot mixture. Add the clams.
Add the scallops and mushrooms, and cook slowly for approximately 45
minutes. Then add the remaining ½ cup of sherry. Adjust the seasonings
again before adding the shrimp, the shellfish (lobster and crab), and cook
for 15 minutes longer. When ready to serve, pour into a large warmed soup
tureen. You are ready to eat a great treat.

SUGGESTED WINE: CHATEAU STE. ROSELINE (ROSÉ PROVENÇE) OR GRENACHE ROSÉ (CALIFORNIA)

SWEET & SOUR MEAT-FILLED
CABBAGE ROLLS

This is a great composition in three parts for a cook who wants to serenade her guests. Cabbage rolls make a hearty feed, best served in winter—but they are most welcome in summer, too, when tender, fresh cabbages are abundant.

Easy to master, even for the beginning cook, they are a great treat for a one-hot-dish buffet dinner, served with a bowl of white rice and a huge mixed green salad. For a Russian touch, serve a bowl of sour cream on the side. They can also be frozen and reheated. Serves 6 to 8.

2 pounds ground beef, round or
 chuck
2 eggs
2 medium onions, finely chopped
¼ cup sugar
Salt and pepper to taste
1 large cabbage
1 tablespoon butter or chicken fat

1 teaspoon sour salt (citric acid)
 dissolved in 1 cup
 cold water
1 large can (20 ounces) tomato
 juice
Salt and pepper
2 small boxes (4 ounces each)
 raisins

HOW TO: Mix the meat, eggs, 2 tablespoons of the chopped onion, 2 teaspoons of the sugar, salt, and pepper, and roll into 16 meat balls, about 1 inch in diameter.

Remove 16 outer leaves of cabbage and parboil, 2 or 3 at a time, in boiling water until semiwilted. This takes about 5 minutes for each set of leaves. With tongs remove the leaves from the boiling water one at a time. Cut out the hard center stem of each leaf to make it more pliable. Set leaves on paper towels to dry before filling with meat.

Meanwhile, prepare sauce. In a large, heavy saucepan sauté the remaining onion in butter or chicken fat until lightly browned. In a small saucepan place the remaining sugar and the sour salt dissolved in water. Cook gently until everything is melted. Pour this mixture into the large saucepan containing the onion, and continue cooking for about 10 minutes, or until onions are a bit browner. Add the tomato juice, half a can at a time, and keep stirring until the mixture is blended. Simmer slowly for about 5 minutes. Season with salt and pepper. Adjust the flavor, adding either more sour salt or more sugar, to get just the right amount of tartness and sweetness to suit your own taste. Then transfer 1 cup of the sauce into a Dutch oven, or enough to cover the bottom.

70

Now fill the cabbage rolls. Take a meat ball and place in the center of a cabbage leaf, folding the sides of the leaf toward the center and then rolling from the base of the leaf to the tip. Gently place cabbage rolls, one at a time, into the Dutch oven so that seamed ends are down and held secure. Arrange the rolls neatly until a layer is completed. Pour another quantity of sauce into the pot, enough to rise above the bottom layer by ½ inch or so. Arrange a second layer of cabbage rolls, another layer of sauce, and so on until all of the cabbage rolls are used up. Cook for 1 ½ hours over low heat. For the last half hour of cooking time, adjust seasonings again and toss raisins on top.

SUGGESTED WINE: EGRI BIKAVER (RED HUNGARIAN) OR CHATEAUNEUF DU PAPE (RED FRENCH RHONE)

ROAST BREAST OF VEAL

Many people characterize certain dishes as "real home cooking" because they seldom see them on restaurant menus. This dish is true "soul food" for most men; they appreciate its tasty, hearty quality. Women like the high yield in praise from the modest investment in time and money. It has paid great dividends in my family for generations.

Breast of veal comes with a natural pocket for the stuffing. Serve it with thinly sliced, orange-flavored steamed carrots or just a salad. Leftovers are tasty served hot or cold. Serves 6 to 8.

5-to-6-pound breast of veal with pocket
1 package (8 ounces) prepared seasoned bread stuffing or 4 cups homemade
1 stalk celery, finely chopped and sautéed
2 tablespoons powdered ginger
2 tablespoons chicken fat

1 small onion, chopped and sautéed
Salt and freshly ground pepper to taste
1 cup cold water
½ cup celery leaves, coarsely chopped
1 small carrot, diced
½ cup dry white wine

HOW TO: Preheat oven to 350° F. Prepare the stuffing. To the stuffing add the chopped celery and half of the chopped onion, both of which have been

71

sautéed. Season the pocket with salt, pepper, and ginger. Fill the pocket with the stuffing, spreading it evenly. Generously rub the outside of the veal with chicken fat and season with additional salt, pepper, and ginger. Put the meat, bone side down, on a rack in the roasting pan. Add a cup of water, the coarsely chopped celery leaves, and the remaining onion and diced carrot. Cover and roast for 2 hours. Remove cover, add the wine, and cook, uncovered, for another hour, or until the meat is nicely browned and tender. Transfer the meat onto a serving platter and slice it in the kitchen, cutting through the bone across the rib top to include the stuffing.

SUGGESTED WINE: SOAVE (DRY WHITE VERONESE)

BAKED NOODLES PARMESAN

Knowing when to use your noodle is important, as every clever hostess knows. Even someone who is not a great cooking buff can master one or two dishes on which to stake her reputation. This recipe is a fine example from a Palm Beach hostess, Esther Goldman. I was lucky to be among her guests when she served this noodle knockout.

It's extremely versatile besides—a fine accompaniment to meat and poultry or an entrée all by itself—and can be made well in advance, frozen, and then reheated at your convenience.

Baked Noodles Parmesan comes out of the oven crisp and golden on top, firm but moist inside, altogether a graceful, neat note for a buffet table. Serves 12 to 14 generously, or cut quantities by half for a smaller dinner party.

2 packages (8 ounces each) fine noodles
¼ pound (1 stick) butter
6 eggs, well beaten

1 cup Parmesan cheese, freshly grated
Salt and white pepper to taste

HOW TO: Preheat oven to 350° F. Boil the noodles in salted water according to package directions and drain well. Melt the butter and add to noodles while still warm. Add the noodles to the beaten eggs. Then add the grated Parmesan cheese. Season with salt and pepper. Butter a flat oven-to-table dish (10"x 15"). Bake for 1 hour. Serve directly from dish, cut into 2-inch-square serving pieces.

Donald Bruce White, one of New York's most sought-after caterers, swaps cooking secrets with me in his professional kitchen at right. The summery dish below is Cucumber Cooler, a recipe featured on page 101.

Summer Salmon Mousse above, lovingly garnished with a garden bouquet and accompanied with a sour cream dressing, is a festive offering from page 18. Momshie's Cookies, left, are crisp, buttery, and plain delicious, on page 83.

Apple Kuchen, an elegant accompaniment for coffee or as a dinner finale, is a Viennese tale told on page 50. Pretty Henny Penny, below, is lovely to look at, delightful to make, and described on page 30.

76

*Two of my favorite culinary
haunts are my own country kitchen,
left, and La Cuisinière, a New
York cookware emporium, above.
Joining me in this photograph is
J. H. Chichester, the genial owner.*

Three stars on the buffet circuit: Apricot Lemon Cake, page 138;
Chaudfroid Vegetables, page 41; and No-Knead French Bread, page 116.

*Exotic sweets for dessert: Baklava, wonderful with honey
and walnuts, page 128; and a party-sized Topless Tart, page 52.*

Herbed Roast Chicken, golden brown and aromatic, as described on page 95.

Smartie Pie, easy does it, with raspberry sauce and whipped cream, page 98.

SWEET NOODLE KUGEL SUPREME

I discovered this savory bit of nostalgia in the refrigerator of Ilo Marcus' home in Armonk, New York. She was expecting her children and grandchildren for a Sunday get-together. I knew there had to be a secret to her calm, unhurried manner. Sure enough, it turned to be her planned-ahead menu—a steak cookout, a salad, and two soufflé bowls filled with this rich pudding. Generous friend that she is, she gave me the recipe without hesitation. It's flawless for all seasons—easily frozen after baking—then defrosted and reheated. Its great value to the hostess lies in the fact that it has to be made 24 hours in advance, *leaving her carefree to enjoy her guests. Serves 12.*

2 packages (8 ounces each) medium-sized noodles
Vegetable oil
12 ounces cream cheese
1 lemon, juice and rind
6 eggs

1 cup sugar
½ pound (2 sticks) butter, melted (reserve 5 tablespoons)
1 pint sour cream
2 heaping cups cornflakes

HOW TO: Prepare the noodles according to package directions. Add a few drops of vegetable oil to the boiling water to prevent sticking. Drain well. In a small bowl mash the cream cheese and add lemon juice and rind. In a large bowl beat the eggs. Add the sugar (less 1 tablespoon) and melted butter (less 5 tablespoons) to the eggs. Add the sour cream and cream cheese-lemon mixture. Combine with the noodles. Mix thoroughly. Place the mixture into a well-buttered casserole (2 small or 1 large). Make a topping of the cornflakes, mixed with 5 tablespoons of cool, melted butter and 1 tablespoon sugar, and sprinkle over the top. Cover the casserole with aluminum foil and refrigerate for 24 hours. When ready to serve, bake at 350° F. for 1 hour. Serve hot or cool.

THE DOUGH THAT BOUGHT TICKETS
AT CARNEGIE HALL

"Sorry, lady, no front seats available for this afternoon's concert. Bernstein's conducting today. The orchestra is sold out. I've only got a few singles left in the second balcony," the man behind the box-office window at Carnegie Hall told my mother.

She was then in her seventies, a short, roly-poly lady. All he could see from his vantage point was her head, which just about reached the window ledge. She wore a perky velour hat, with a veil tightly drawn across it, just clearing her pudgy little nose. She looked up, cocked her head at a flirtatious tilt, and said. "Are you sure there isn't just one seat up front? I never miss one of Lenny's concerts. I don't hear very well, so I don't mind sitting in the first row. Please check again—maybe somebody's returned a ticket. In the meantime, have a cookie. I bring these with me to have a bite with a cup of tea during intermission. I make them myself. I think you'll like them."

"Thanks, lady, but I can't promise anything. Maybe something will turn up in half an hour. Come back later and I'll see what I can do for you."

My mother headed for the Russian Tea Room next door to enjoy lunching with a friend in anticipation of the concert—pleased with the success of her maneuver. When she returned, a ticket for a good seat did turn up somehow.

I heard this story from her some months later, when I stopped by her apartment, just as she was leaving for a concert. She was carrying a small, gaily wrapped package. "Sorry I can't stay, but I'm on my way to Carnegie Hall," she said as she brushed by me, heading for the elevator.

I asked what she was carrying in the package. "Oh, that!" she replied, "I'm taking my cookies to the box-office man at Carnegie Hall—he loves them—when I go to buy a ticket he always finds a good seat for me!"

This arrangement lasted happily for several years until she died. When the new Philharmonic Hall (now Avery Fisher) was built at Lincoln Center, we dedicated a seat in her memory. Music was one of her passions. I like to think of her sitting up front on Friday matinees, enjoying the performance.

MOMSHIE'S COOKIES

Because these cookies are the first delicious sweet I can re-member eating, never having tasted their equal anywhere, I consider them the most valuable of my family treasures.

My mother told me what ingredients she used, but I ne-glected to record them in a formal recipe. It took years of tin-kering with the proportions to achieve the correct quantities. Do I dare say mine are even better? Certainly I can promise that if you follow the recipe your cookies will turn out just as good as hers were. (See color photograph on page 74.) Makes 36 cookies.

¼ **pound (1 stick) butter, sweet or salted**
1 **scant cup sugar**
1 **whole large egg**
1 **large egg, separated**
1 **teaspoon vanilla extract**
1 **cup unbleached flour**

½ **teaspoon baking powder**
2 **tablespoons chopped walnuts mixed with a little cinnamon and sugar**
1 **dozen almond halves**
2 **tablespoons raspberry jam or orange marmalade**

HOW TO MAKE: Put the butter and sugar in a mixing bowl and chop them together with 2 forks (this will prevent the butter from becoming too soft) until the mixture is crumbled to the size of small peas. *Do not use a spoon, a beater, or your hands.* Add the whole egg and continue to mix with a

wooden spoon. Add the yolk of the separated egg and the vanilla extract and continue mixing until the dough is well blended and is the consistency of a soft cereal, but not too smooth. (Store the egg white in a small jar in the refrigerator to use as a glaze when you are ready to bake the cookies.)

Sift the flour and baking powder together and slowly add to the butter-sugar-egg mixture. Stir the dough gently until all the flour is absorbed. Do not handle with fingers. Ease the dough out of the bowl onto a large piece of Saran wrap or aluminum foil, scraping the sides of the bowl with a rubber spatula. Place the wrapped dough in the refrigerator for a minimum of 5 hours or overnight, or even a day or two in the freezer compartment, until you are ready to bake the cookies. The preparation of the dough takes 15 minutes.

HOW TO BAKE: Preheat oven to 350° F. Lightly butter two large cookie sheets. Remove the dough from the refrigerator and with fingers form into marble-sized balls (about ¾ inch). Place on the cookie sheet 1 inch apart and flatten each with the palm of your hand. Remove the egg white from the refrigerator and beat lightly. With a pastry brush gently glaze the tops of the cookies. Decorate with a bit of the cinnamon-nut-sugar mixture or an almond half placed in the center. Make a small indentation in the center of the cookie when you dot with the jelly or marmalade. Bake for 10 minutes until they are a delicate golden color. Remove the pan from the oven and with a spatula *immediately* lift the cookies onto a serving dish. Do not leave to cool on the pan because they harden quickly.

To bake two trays at a time, place the first tray on the lower shelf for 5 minutes, then switch it to the top shelf for another 5 minutes—inserting the second tray on the bottom shelf at this point.

INDIVIDUAL CHEESECAKES

*This recipe is my idea of "the living end in deliciousness."
The great fun here is to offer cheesecake in individual servings,
without slicing, for buffet service. These can be stored easily
and can be used in emergencies as needed, without taking up
the space of a large-sized cake. Makes 12 individual cheesecakes.*

6 Holland rusks, crushed
6 tablespoons butter, melted
12 fluted paper or aluminum muffin
   liners
2 packages (8 ounces each) cream
   cheese at room temperature

¾ cup plus 2 tablespoons sugar
1 teaspoon vanilla extract
½ teaspoon cream of tartar
3 eggs
2½ teaspoons lemon juice
1 pint sour cream

HOW TO: Preheat oven to 350° F. Mix together the crushed rusks and melted butter. Place fluted liners in a muffin tin and cover bottom of each with ⅛ inch of rusk-butter mixture, saving enough (about 2 tablespoons) to sprinkle on top later. Place in the oven and bake for about 10 minutes, or until a crust is formed. Take care not to burn the crust.

Meanwhile, prepare the cheese mixture. Soften the cream cheese in a bowl. Add ¾ cup of sugar, vanilla extract, and cream of tartar. Beat the hell out of it until it's very light—or use electric mixer or beater. Add the eggs, one at a time, and continue beating. Add the lemon juice. Whip ferociously. Pour the mixture into pastry cups, filling each ¾ of the way. Return muffin tin to oven and bake for 15 minutes. Remove from the oven and let cool. Mix the sour cream with the 2 tablespoons of sugar and fill remainder of each cup with sour cream. Sprinkle the top with a few rusk crumbs and return to oven for 8 minutes more of baking. Let stand in pan until cooled and comfortable to handle. Remove cheesecake cups and place on serving platter or store in the refrigerator until needed.

O'CONNOR'S JUICED APPLE PIE

To Bill O'Connor of Tarrytown, New York, baking is a great hobby. For my money, this is a perfect pie from start to finish.

The secret is to keep the juices that usually bubble out of and over the pie crust inside, where they belong. A more flavorful pie and a neater oven is the result. To do this, Tarrytown's master pieman sprinkles sugar on the raw apple slices and leaves them to stand in a bowl to exude their juices. The drained apples are baked in a double crust, and when the pie is done, the liquid, somewhat transformed in the interim, is poured into holes in the top crust of the pie.

The pie may be made a day or two ahead of time, refrigerated, and then left to stand at room temperature the day you plan to use it. Serves 6 to 8.

6 large green apples	**1 cup solid white vegetable**
1¼ cups sugar	**shortening**
1 teaspoon cinnamon	**¼ cup ice water**
⅛ teaspoon nutmeg	**2 tablespoons flour or 1½**
¼ teaspoon salt	**teaspoons tapioca (Minute**
2 cups sifted unbleached flour	**brand)**
1 teaspoon salt	**3 tablespoons butter**

HOW TO: Peel, core, and slice the apples. Combine the sugar, cinnamon, nutmeg, and salt, and coat the apples with the mixture. Let stand for at least 2 hours. Drain the apples and reserve the syrup that forms.

Meanwhile, make the pie crust. Sift the flour and salt into a mixing bowl and cut in the shortening, using a pastry blender or 2 knives. Add the ice water gradually, tossing the mixture with a 2-prong fork. Shape the dough into a ball, handling the dough as little as possible.

Preheat oven to 450° F. On a lightly floured base roll out half the dough and line a 9-inch pie plate. Arrange the apple slices on top of the pastry and pack closely, letting them pile up until pie is full. Roll out the remaining dough and cut 2 holes near the center, each about the size of a dime. Wet the rim of the bottom crust. Cover with top crust and trim and crimp the edges. Bake for 45 minutes until golden. Let cool slightly. Meanwhile, put drained syrup in a saucepan and stir in the flour or the tapioca and the butter. Bring to a boil. Pour this syrup into the 2 holes through a small funnel. Serve at room temperature.

Take Hot Tips!

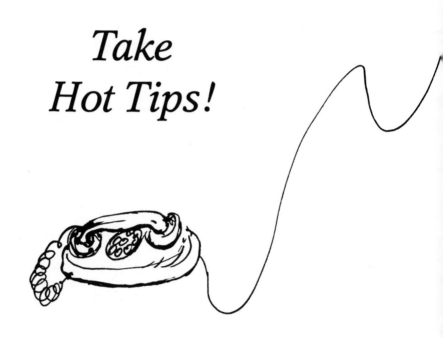

RIDE WITH A WINNER

Bet on the basics when you're a beginner,
Make Perfect Rice to ride with a winner.
A cold minted soup lifts up underachievers,
A whole Herbed Chicken is for gay deceivers.

You'll welcome the ease of Lamb in a Stew,
You'll thrill to the taste of a Coconut Chew.
A Smartie Pie is what pure bliss is,
Sure to be followed by fervent kisses.

LINGUINI CON MASCHERPONE E NOCE

One of the newest restaurants in Georgetown, that charming enclave of international intrigue on the edge of Washington, D.C., caters to V.I.P.'s and is aptly named The Big Cheese. It specializes in unusual cheese concoctions gathered from around the world. When I tasted this delicate pasta at brunch I realized it might be easy to duplicate at home.

A blend of cheeses makes the sauce. Sprinkle chopped walnuts on top, and Presto!—you have a marvelous main course to serve with a crisp green salad and crusty French bread (see recipe on page 116).

The owners were kind enough to reveal the secret—quite simple as it turns out—of this delectable dish. Serves 4.

1 package (8 ounces) linguini (thin pasta ribbons)
2 quarts water
2 packages (8 ounces each) Borden's Lite-Line Neufchatel cream cheese

1 cup heavy cream (or half-and-half)
1 cup freshly grated Parmesan cheese
Salt to taste
½ cup walnuts, chopped
Freshly ground black pepper to taste

HOW TO: Bring the lightly salted water to a rolling boil and cook the linguini until *al dente* (just tender). Drain off the liquid, but do not run cold water over the pasta. Divide the linguini into equal serving portions and put into individual warmed soup plates.

While the water is boiling prepare the sauce so that it will be ready to serve when the pasta is done. Put the cream cheese and the cream into a blender and blend till smooth, but not frothy, 3 seconds. Remove from the blender and add the grated Parmesan cheese. Place the mixture in the top of a double boiler and heat for about 5 minutes, until well blended. Season with salt. Pour the sauce over the pasta. Sprinkle the chopped walnuts on top. Pass a pepper mill for those who like the taste of freshly ground pepper.

SUGGESTED WINE: ORVIETO (DRY WHITE, WELL-CHILLED)

PLAICIE'S SCOTCH BROTH

Pipe in the whole clan to enjoy a hearty, thrifty meal in a bowl. This barley soup was included in a book published to honor Margaret Plaicie on her nineteenth birthday in 1970. Pamela Johnson of Sussex, England, who knew this famous cook's repertoire, explained that as a young girl Plaicie studied with the great French and English chefs of the Victorian era. She was also a devotee of English poetry, and the combination was enchanting. She developed her great creative talents to become a poetess in the kitchen. Serves 6.

2 lamb shanks
1 ½ quarts cold water
1 cup barley
3 carrots, cut into ½-inch slices
2 leeks, sliced crosswise (whites only)

2 medium-sized white turnips, peeled and quartered
Salt and pepper to taste
1 teaspoon rosemary, powdered

HOW TO: Bring 1 ½ quarts of lightly salted water to a boil. Put in the lamb shanks and barley, and simmer, covered, for 1 ½ hours. Then add the carrots, leeks, and turnips, and boil gently for an additional ½ hour. Season with salt, pepper, and rosemary. Remove the shanks, cut away any fat and meat left on them, discard the fat, and return the meat to the broth.

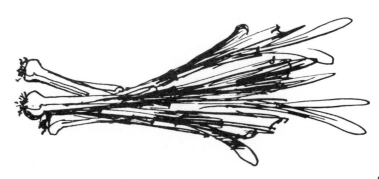

EVER-READY FRENCH DRESSING

Juggling bottles of oil, vinegar, and salad seasonings before guests may be a nice curtain raiser for that very special salad, but often it's just one more bit of table clutter that is better dispensed with. You could, of course, get the same degree of freshness working behind the scene in the kitchen just moments before serving, but who wants to stop for that when there are so many things to do.

An experienced homemaker, Nathalie Finkelstein of Scarsdale, New York, prefers to make her subtle dressing in advance and store it in the refrigerator; miracle of miracles, there is no sacrifice in flavor.

Follow her advice and you will be insured against being caught undressed—your salad, that is—at any important meal. I keep a jar of dressing on hand, occasionally adding a bit of Roquefort cheese or fines herbes for variety. Makes 1 cup.

1 teaspoon salt
½ teaspoon black pepper
¼ teaspoon dry mustard
1 clove garlic, minced

2 tablespoons wine vinegar, red or white
1 cup olive oil

HOW TO: Combine all the ingredients in a jar, cover, and shake well. Store in the refrigerator. Remove a few minutes before using, shake, and sprinkle over salad as needed.

EGGPLANT & MUSHROOM PIE

Though the word for eggplant sounds more mellifluous in French as aubergine, *or in Italian as* melanzana, *eggplant in plain English is still a soul-satisfying sight. Here is a bonanza for those who are attracted to the deep-purple sheen and rich flavor of this beautiful vegetable. Among this dish's advantages are its ease of preparation and its versatility—it can be served as an hors d'oeuvre or as a hot appetizer baked in a quiche dish for a cold buffet. Also, it can be made days or weeks in advance, refrigerated or frozen, and reheated when needed. Men especially seem to enjoy its zesty flavor.*

Mary Lou Donarski, from the Duchy of Luxembourg and South Salem, New York, is the custodian who guards this treasure. Serves 10 for hors d'oeuvres or 4 to 6 as a main-course vegetable.

1 medium-sized eggplant, unpeeled (cut into 1-inch-thick semicircles, 2 cups total)
¼ pound (1 stick) butter
1 cup fresh mushrooms, coasely chopped
½ cup celery leaves, chopped

1 clove garlic, minced
½ teaspoon seasoned salt
1 teaspoon mixed salad herbs (Spice Islands brand)
¼ cup tomato paste
1 8-inch pastry shell, homemade or ready-frozen

HOW TO: Preheat oven to 475° F. Cut the eggplant in half and then cut into 1-inch-thick semicircles. In a covered skillet sauté the eggplant in butter for 10 minutes over low heat, turning once or twice. Add the mushrooms, celery leaves, and garlic, and sauté until the mushrooms begin to wilt, stirring constantly. Add the seasonings and tomato paste. Stir once to mix, and turn the mixture into the unbaked pie shell. Bake for 45 to 50 minutes until the filling is bubbling and the crust is brown. Cool slightly before serving.

MODZOUN SOUP—MINTED TREASURE

Even though you may be a neophyte in the kitchen, don't limit yourself to commonplace fare. Here is an exotic summer soup to serve very well chilled. It may be prepared several days ahead of time and kept in the refrigerator, to be used when the occasion arises.

Armenian by birth, it has a subtle, minty flavor. It's great for dieters, as it does not call for the heavy cream, flour, or butter that usually go into creamy soups.

Ciel Thurman of Somers, New York, is the kind of venturesome hostess who enjoys traveling unchartered culinary seas. Thanks to her, you and I can sally forth, under her expert guidance. Serves 6.

½ cup barley
6 cups chicken broth
2 tablespoons onion, finely chopped and sautéed
½ cup fresh mint leaves, finely chopped

3 containers (8 ounces each) plain yogurt
¾ teaspoon salt
Salt and pepper to taste

HOW TO: Place the barley in a small pan, cover with cold water, and let soak overnight. When ready to use, rinse well and drain. Put the chicken broth in a medium-sized saucepan, add the barley, bring to a boil, and then let simmer 15 minutes, until barley is tender. Sauté the onion in a little butter until browned, then add to the soup. Add the chopped mint and let steep—do not cook. When the mixture has cooled to room temperature, add the yogurt, salt, and pepper. Chill well. When ready to serve, pour the soup into chilled bowls. Serve with freshly ground black pepper.

FISH SOUFFLÉ—THE BLENDER WAY

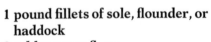

The original recipe comes from Curtis Taylor, a Purchase, New York, graduate student with a highly cultivated palate and limited funds. It is a great penny-pinching dish for entertaining.

Simple ingredients, satisfying delicate flavors, effortless preparation—all mixed in one flick of the blender. You just can't flub this. The soufflé works as a main course for lunch or dinner, or as an elegant entrée for a more formal event. It may be made well in advance of serving and warmed before eating. Serves 4.

1 pound fillets of sole, flounder, or haddock
2 tablespoons flour
5 tablespoons softened butter
1 teaspoon salt
Pinch of pepper
⅛ teaspoon fresh or dried tarragon or grated nutmeg

¾ cup light cream or half-and-half
1 egg white
2 shallots, chopped fine
½ cup fresh mushrooms, chopped
2 tablespoons white wine (preferably Sauterne)
1 tablespoon parsley, finely chopped

HOW TO: Preheat oven to 250° F. Cut the fish fillets into tiny ½-inch pieces. Drain and discard all liquid. Put the fish, 1 tablespoon of flour, 3 tablespoons of butter, seasonings, and ½ cup of cream into a blender, making sure to saturate all layers with cream. Blend thoroughly at low speed, about 5 minutes in all. The mixture should be quite heavy, like mashed potatoes. Hand-beat egg white separately until stiff. Remove the fish mixture from the blender and fold in the egg white. Place in a buttered loaf pan or an oval oven-to-table serving dish. Bake until center is firm (toothpick test), about ½ hour.

Sauté the shallots and mushrooms in the remaining 2 tablespoons of butter over low heat. Add 1 tablespoon of flour, remaining ¼ cup light cream, and wine. Blend together until smooth. Pour this sauce over the fish when ready to serve. Sprinkle with chopped parsley.

SUGGESTED WINE: MEURSAULT (ELEGANT WHITE BURGUNDY)

PERFECT RICE

It took me years to master the art of making plain cooked rice. I either had the wrong pot, or one without a tight enough cover, or I cooked it too fast or too slow. In any case, it came out a mushy mess or way underdone instead of perfectly cooked with grains separated, the way I like it. Without any reservation I can say this way to prepare rice in the oven guarantees perfect rice at all times. It works equally well for brown rice or wild rice. You can substitute clear chicken broth or tomato juice for the water. You can add finely chopped onions or peppers, or any other type of vegetable appropriate to the particular dish that accompanies it — a bit of curry powder or soy sauce for a Chinese dish, and so on.

It can be served in the dish it's made in as nothing boils over or sticks to the bottom. The idea comes from the same Ronnie Kaufman of Santa Monica, California, who took the photographs in this book. Blessings. Serves 4 to 6.

2½ cups boiling water
1 cup raw white rice
2 tablespoons butter
Pinch of salt

HOW TO: Preheat oven to 300° F. Butter the casserole. Place all of the ingredients in an uncovered casserole and bake for 45 to 60 minutes, stirring once or twice during the process.

BEEF WITH MUSHROOMS & SOUR CREAM

You deserve a break today, so get up and get away from McDonald's. Here's a quick and easy stroganov, as tasty as its elegant cousin made with fancy tenderloin. It takes about ½ hour to prepare and ½ hour to cook. You can refrigerate or freeze it. Great to serve over broad noodles. Thanks to Robert C. Ackart, opera buff and cookbook author of Katonah, New York, for another easy way to make this main-course treat. Serves 6, can be doubled.

4 tablespoons butter
2 or 3 onions, minced
2 pounds ground beef
2 cloves garlic sliced lengthwise
4 tablespoons flour
¾ teaspoon salt
¼ teaspoon white pepper

½ pound mushrooms, sliced lengthwise
1 can cream of mushroom soup, undiluted
1 cup sour cream
Fresh dill or parsley

HOW TO: In a 6-quart casserole melt the butter and cook the onion until translucent. Add the meat and garlic, and cook, stirring, until lightly browned. Stir in the flour, salt, and pepper. Add the mushrooms. Cover and cook for 5 minutes. Stir in the mushroom soup and simmer, covered, for 10 minutes. Add the sour cream to the simmering casserole, stirring. Reduce heat and warm through—do not cook further. Before serving, sprinkle with fresh dill or parsley.

SUGGESTED WINE: ST. EMILION (FRUITY RED BORDEAUX) OR RUBY CABERNET (CALIFORNIA)

Rosemary

Tarragon

HERBED ROAST CHICKEN
NO BASTE—NO WASTE

This recipe guarantees a delicious result even if it is your first venture in roasting a chicken. The real secret is high heat, to seal in the juices and eliminate the nuisance of basting. It is equally tasty whether served hot or cold, in a festive setting or in a picnic basket. It can be prepared two or three days in advance, frozen, and then reheated when needed. It takes exactly 3 minutes to prepare and 1 hour to cook.

To vary the flavor, try altering the herb mixture: leave out the garlic and use a sprinkling of ready-mixed fines herbes, or perhaps a dash of powdered ginger, or ⅛ teaspoon of powdered cloves to give a wonderful East Indian lift, or omit the salt for special diets, and it's still tasty. (See color photograph on page 80.) Serves 4 to 6.

1 fatty roasting chicken,
  4 to 5 pounds
   (or a 3- to 3½-pound fryer)
Salt and pepper to taste

2 cloves garlic, minced
2 to 3 tablespoons tarragon
  or rosemary, fresh or dried
1 large whole onion

HOW TO: Preheat oven to 450° F. Season the chicken and cavity with salt and pepper. Sprinkle the outside with minced fresh garlic. Place 2 to 3 tablespoons fresh or dried tarragon or rosemary in the cavity and add the onion. Place the chicken in a Dutch oven or heavy pot. Roast, tightly covered, for 1 hour for a large chicken, 45 minutes for a smaller chicken. Remove the cover during the last 5 minutes if the chicken needs additional browning. Skin should be crisp and nicely browned. Transfer to a warm serving dish.

SUGGESTED WINE: POUILLY FUISSÉ (WHITE BURGUNDY) OR PINOT CHARDONNAY (CALIFORNIA)

LAMB WORTH GETTING INTO A STEW ABOUT

This dish seems to be the all-time favorite of my friends, perhaps because it is a universally nostalgic, homey affair. Unfortunately, the preparation of a good lamb stew seems to elude many. This one is not only simple, it has a brighter flavor than most because it uses white turnips instead of potatoes. Also, it is as fat-free as a lamb dish can be. The casserole can be frozen and reheated, assuring you a wonderful leftover dish whenever you choose to have it, and like some marriages, it is better the second time around. Serve it with white rice or medium-sized noodles and a green salad. Serves 6.

4 to 5 pounds shank or shoulder lamb chops, cut into 2-inch pieces
Salt and pepper to taste
2 tablespoons flour
1 cup tomato sauce, thinned with 1 cup hot water, or 2 cups tomato juice
1 bunch carrots, scraped and cut into 2-inch lengths

12 small fresh white onions (not canned, please)
1 bay leaf
½ teaspoon rosemary, powdered
2 white turnips, peeled and diced
1 package (10 ounces) frozen peas
2 tablespoons parsley, chopped

HOW TO: In a 6-quart Dutch oven with a cover, brown the lamb well on all sides. There is enough fat in the lamb so no extra fat is required. Sprinkle with salt, pepper, and flour. Add the tomato sauce in hot water or the tomato juice. Cover and cook for about 30 minutes over medium heat. Add bayleaf and rosemary, and cook slowly for another hour, or until lamb is tender. Remove from heat and empty into a large bowl. Store at least for 3 hours, or overnight, in the refrigerator to allow the fat to congeal. When

96

ready to serve, remove and discard all fat. Steam the carrots, turnips, and onions in one large pot, until just fork tender. Steam the peas in a separate pot. Place all the vegetables in a bowl until you want to serve the stew. Put the lamb and vegetables together into a stove-to-table casserole, reheat till bubbling, adjust seasonings, and serve sprinkled with chopped parsley.

SUGGESTED WINE: BEAUJOLAIS (LIGHT RED BURGUNDY). CAMAY NOIR (CALIFORNIA)

COCONUT CHEWS

These delectable morsels are a tradition in many families. They are called "Best in the World," or "B-W's" for short, by members of the Miron family, a large clan that lives in New Jersey.

Coconut Chews take 10 minutes to prepare and ½ hour to bake, are sure-fire male bait, irresistible and habit forming—the perfect go-along with fruit or coffee. They will keep a week, if given the chance. Makes 49 coconut chews or 2 pounds for a modest $1, even at today's prices—a real buy!

¼ **pound (1 stick) butter at room temperature**
2 cups dark brown sugar
1 cup flour, sifted
2 eggs
1 teaspoon vanilla extract

½ **canned shredded coconut mixed with**
2 tablespoons flour
½ **cup walnuts, chopped**
Confectioners' sugar

HOW TO: Preheat oven to 350° F. In a bowl blend together the butter, 1 cup of the sugar, and flour. This is easily done with an electric beater, or if you like, you can mush the mixture with your hands. Pat down in ungreased square pan (8"x8") and bake for 15 minutes. Meanwhile, beat 2 eggs well, add the other cup of sugar, vanilla extract, and blend. Fold in the walnuts and coconut (which has been blended with 2 tablespoons flour to prevent coconut shreds from sticking together).

Remove the pan from the oven and pour the egg mixture over the baked crust. Bake for an additional 10 to 15 minutes until top is firm, but not too brown. Let cool a bit. Then cut into squares—score it six times across, six times down. Remove to a serving platter or cake plate, and when cool, sift the confectioners' sugar on top.

SMARTIE PIE

Sam Levenson, the well-known humorist, likes to tell stories about his mother, a lady with a gift for cool improvisation. When, for example, she dropped an egg on the floor, she would say, "Well, I think I'll bake a cake." Whenever I find a number of broken Ritz crackers in the box, I immediately decide to bake a Smartie Pie.

This dish is a delight, because it looks so elegant, so professional, and yet it is so inexpensive that it makes the hostess feel like a real "Smartie Pie." Nobody, but nobody, seems to guess how this is put together. Certainly not me the first time I tasted it.

Baffle your guests while you enjoy the pleasure of being an overachiever. (See color photograph on page 80.) Serves 6.

3 egg whites	20 broken and crumbled Ritz
1 teaspoon baking powder	crackers (do not pulverize)
1 cup sugar	½ pint whipped cream
1 teaspoon vanilla extract	2 tablespoons sugar
¾ cup walnuts, chopped	1 package frozen raspberries or
	strawberries in syrup

HOW TO: Preheat oven to 325° F. Grease a 9-inch pie pan or quiche dish. With an electric hand-beater beat the egg whites until stiff, slowly adding the baking powder, 1 cup of sugar, and vanilla extract. When well blended, fold in the walnuts and crumbled Ritz crackers. Pour into the pie pan, bake for 30 minutes until firm (use toothpick test). It should not be brown, but set. Serve with raspberries or strawberries and whipped cream, to which 2 tablespoons of sugar has been added.

7

Cool It!

BEAT THE HEAT

In the summer when the weather's sublime,
Free yourself—don't waste any time.
Chill a Gazpacho or a Shrimp Mousse,
This is the time to put greens to good use.

Set chicken or lamb in a fine marinade,
Swing in a hammock and sip lemonade.
Chill a Bean Salad, then go for a swim,
Remember to leave the cooking to him.

GAZPACHO LAURENT

Feel like a gypsy sometimes? Want to roam the woods and leave all domestic responsibility behind? Fix a wonderful Spanish soup to keep on hand in the refrigerator for just such times. This variation of the Iberian favorite comes from Bernice Newman of North Stamford, Connecticut, a well-organized hostess and busy executive. She keeps her cool with minimal effort. This is a delightful way to use summer fresh products from the garden. The blender does all the work. Serves 4.

1 medium onion, chopped
1 clove garlic, crushed
5 very ripe tomatoes, peeled and
  chopped
3 parsley sprigs, chopped

3 tablespoons vinegar
1 tablespoon olive oil
1 cup cold beef consommé
Salt and pepper to taste

Garnishes
½ cup tomatoes, chopped
½ cup green peppers, chopped
½ cup scallions, chopped

½ cup cucumbers, chopped
½ cup white bread croutons

HOW TO: Put the onion and garlic into a blender to liquefy. Add the other ingredients and run the blender for 2 or 3 minutes. Season with salt and pepper. Pour the contents into a jar and store it in the refrigerator to chill. When ready to serve, pour the soup into a chilled tureen or individual chilled soup plates. Place the garnishes in a sectioned dish for guests to choose.

SHRIMP MOUSSE

Here's a pretty how-d'ya-do. The pink color of shrimp in aspic, trimmed with crisp greens, brings a country garden indoors. A few minutes of preparation, and you are free to enjoy the day. For an attractive presentation, this light and tasty dish can be served for lunch or embellished with vegetables or hard-cooked eggs to become the centerpiece for a summer buffet. Serves 6.

1 envelope unflavored gelatin
⅓ cup cold water
1 can (10 ounces) tomato soup,
  undiluted
1 package (8 ounces) cream cheese
  at room temperature

Dressing
½ pint sour cream
1 teaspoon fresh dill,
  finely chopped

1 pound medium shrimp, peeled,
  shelled, and deveined
1 cup celery, chopped
½ cup onion, chopped
¼ cup prepared mayonnaise

1 teaspoon fresh chives, finely
  chopped
2 tablespoons cucumber, peeled,
  seeded, and finely chopped

HOW TO: Dissolve the gelatin in water. Bring the tomato soup to a boil, then turn off the heat. Add the gelatin to the soup, stirring well. Add the softened cream cheese and blend thoroughly. Let cool and add the shrimp, celery, onion, and mayonnaise.

Pour into a lightly oiled 1½-quart decorative mold. Leave in the refrigerator overnight to set. To unmold the mousse, place the mold in a pan filled with lukewarm water for a minute to loosen, and invert onto a serving dish. Decorate with greens or the other imaginative embellishments you have prepared and stored in a bowl of iced water. Keep in the refrigerator until just before serving time.

SUGGESTED WINE: RIESLING (WHITE GRAPEY ALSACE) OR GREY RIESLING (CALIFORNIA)

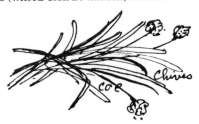

CUCUMBER COOLER

Just the sight of a chilled cucumber soup is refreshing. (See color photograph on page 73.) This creamed soup is made without flour. Though it requires a few moments at stove side in the morning, it's worth it for the marvelous cool taste at lunch or dinner. It can be kept chilled for several days in the refrigerator. Credit for this fine summer treat goes to Theresa A. Morse of Martha's Vineyard, Massachusetts. Serves 6.

101

4 tablespoons scallions or shallots or onions, chopped	3 tablespoons uncooked cream of wheat
2 tablespoons butter	Salt and white pepper to taste
2 long thin cucumbers, peeled, seeded, and cut into small chunks	2 or 3 drops green vegetable coloring
1 teaspoon white wine vinegar	½ cup sour cream
1 teaspoon lemon juice	2 tablespoons fresh chives, chopped
1 quart chicken broth	2 tablespoons fresh parsley, chopped
1 teaspoon fresh dill chopped	

HOW TO: Cook the scallions or shallots or onions in the butter until soft. Add the cucumbers, vinegar, lemon juice, chicken broth, and dill. Bring to a boil and add the cream of wheat. Simmer, uncovered, for 30 minutes. Put the contents through a strainer, allowing the liquid to drip into a bowl. The solid ingredients left in the strainer go into the blender with a few tablespoons of the soup liquid. Blend for 30 seconds. Return the contents of the blender to the soup. Season with salt and pepper and add the green coloring. When slightly cooled, add the sour cream and mix thoroughly. Before serving, top with chopped chives and parsley. This soup is best very cold and served in chilled bowls.

JUNGLE GREEN SALAD

While I have listed this salad as a cooler, it's agreeable, satisfying, and nourishing all year round. It will make you feel virtuous after a few days of gourmandizing on richer foods. The New York Health Club features it on its menu—and they ought to know what's slimming. Serves 1.

3 raw whole spinach leaves
3 pieces of Romaine lettuce
3 sprigs watercress with stems
3 slivers red cabbage
3 slivers celery
1 teaspoon red pepper, diced
1 teaspoon green pepper, diced
2 slices fresh pineapple
1 cup alfalfa sprouts

1 teaspoon dried sunflower seeds
1 teaspoon Quaker Oats natural
  cereal
4 or 5 cubes of Cheddar cheese
4 or 5 cubes of Jarlsberg cheese
Fresh lemon juice
Veg-Sel
Kelp powder } health-food products

HOW TO: In a salad bowl toss the raw vegetables, pineapple, alfalfa sprouts, sunflower seeds, cereals, and cheeses. Sprinkle with the lemon juice, Veg-Sel, and kelp powder.

CHICK PEAS RÉMOULADE

When waves of guests begin to inundate your house on summer weekends, use your bean. You can remain cool and convivial in such emergencies if you have on hand this appetizing refreshment. It has a salty tang that goes well with long thirst-quenching drinks. No cooking needed for this, so you can assemble it a day or two ahead of time. Keep it in the refrigerator—ready to be snapped up by hungry guests. Serves 6.

3 flat anchovy fillets
1 clove garlic, crushed
1 tablespoon capers, chopped
1 teaspoon shallots, minced
2 tablespoons parsley, minced

½ cup mayonnaise
Salt and pepper to taste
Lemon juice to taste (about
  1 tablespoon)
1 large can (20 ounces) chick peas

HOW TO: In a small bowl (I use a mortar and pestle for this) blend the anchovies, garlic, capers, shallots, and parsley. Mix into the mayonnaise and season with salt, pepper, and lemon juice. Drain the chick peas thoroughly and add the seasoned mayonnaise. Store in the refrigerator in a covered jar. When ready to serve, transfer to a decorative dish with or without greens.

SEAFOOD 'N' SHELLS

Reminiscent of sun and surf at the shore, minus burns and sand, is this tasty one-dish mixture of seafood and pasta shells. You can cook the shells early in the morning or a day before. You can then go off to the beach with the knowledge that a satisfying meal can be assembled in minutes when you get back home. If it rains, serve Seafood 'n' Shells anyway, as a consolation. How's that for being a Pollyanna?

If you are near a shore resort, you probably know the whereabouts of a fresh fish market and can pick up shelled clams or cleaned shrimp—ready to go. If not, or if you like to stockpile your larder to be ready for hungry drop-ins, keep cans of whole clams and some quick frozen shrimp on hand.

A tossed green salad with an oil and vinegar dressing is a fine companion. I discovered this casserole at the home of Leonore Baronio, a busy Westchester landscape designer, of Rye, New York, known for her good taste both indoors and out. Serves 6.

8 ounces pasta shells (½ package Ronzoni #21, or equivalent)
4 tablespoons butter
¼ cup olive oil
4 cloves garlic, minced
1 cup onion, finely chopped
½ teaspoon salt
Black pepper, to taste
¼ cup parsley, finely chopped

1 package (10 ounces) frozen baby peas (petits pois)
1 can (8 ounces) whole shelled clams or minced clams in white sauce
½ pound fresh shrimp, shelled and boiled
Parmesan cheese, grated

HOW TO: Cook the shells according to package directions in lightly salted water. Don't forget to include a drop or two of oil to prevent the pasta from sticking. When cooked *al dente*, which means "tender to the tooth," drain under cold water and set aside in a bowl.

Preheat oven to 350° F. In a skillet melt the butter and olive oil. Add the garlic and chopped onion, and brown until golden. Mix together with the pasta shells. Season with salt and pepper. Put into a well-buttered casserole, add the chopped parsley, and toss lightly. You can set the casserole overnight in the refrigerator. Cook the frozen peas in ½ cup of boiling water for about 5 minutes; when ready add to the casserole. Fifteen minutes before serving, add the clam sauce or whole clams and boiled shrimp, mix carefully with pasta shells, heat in the oven for about 15 minutes until thoroughly heated. Serve with grated Parmesan cheese on the side.

SUGGESTED WINE: STEINWEIN (WHITE FRUITY GERMAN IN *BOXBEUTEL*, OR FLASK)

KEEN BEAN SALAD

If your kitchen sometimes seems like a mess hall in summer, here's a clever way to feed the crowd during steamy weather. If possible, make this salad at least two days in advance in preparation for the weekend, for instance, to allow the dressing and seasonings to thoroughly permeate the mixture. Thanks to Dr. Sylvia L. Gennis of New Rochelle, New York, who gave me the idea for this handsome salad she serves to the guests who turn up around her pool—she now suspects that some people come for the salad and enjoy the pool as an afterthought. Serves 10 to 12.

1 can (20 ounces) red kidney beans
1 can (20 ounces) chick peas
1 can (16 ounces) cut green beans
1 can (20 ounces) white kidney beans (cannellini)
3 scallions, finely chopped (green tops included)
1 jar (4 ounces) pimentos, chopped
2 cucumbers, peeled and diced
3 cloves garlic, minced
½ cup parsley, finely chopped
1 can (8 ounces) pitted black olives
Salt and pepper to taste
½ cup good French dressing (see recipe on page 90)

HOW TO: Thoroughly drain all the cans of beans. Place the contents into one large bowl. Mix in all the other ingredients, stir well, and store in the refrigerator for 2 days. Stir once or twice during this period. Serve well chilled in a large bowl.

VEGETARIAN VICTUALS

With so many people on meatless diets, it behooves a modern hostess to include a hearty, interesting vegetarian dish in her repertoire. This glamorous meal-in-a-dish was created by Milton Williams, the California caterer to a host of hostesses in Hollywood. It's ideal hot-weather cold fare, and the longer it sits, the better it gets. So make it at least a few days before you plan to serve it. If you mean to be strictly vegetarian with it, top with sliced hard-boiled eggs. For guests who feel otherwise, serve separately a topping of shrimp or tuna or shredded cold chicken. Serves 8 generously.

1 package (10 ounces) frozen green peas
1 package (10 ounces) frozen whole cut green beans
8 small new potatoes, diced, (total 4 cups)
3 cups chicken stock or broth
½ cup green pepper, finely chopped
½ cup radishes, finely chopped
1 cup celery, finely chopped
1 cup scallions, finely chopped (including green tops)
1 cup water chestnuts, slivered
2 teaspoons salt
2 cloves garlic, minced
3 tablespoons Durkees Famous Sauce (mustard dressing)
2 tablespoons mayonnaise
½ cup sour cream
1 small onion, grated
1 tablespoon dill, finely chopped
Salt and pepper to taste
1 cup French dressing (see recipe on page 90)

HOW TO: Cook the packaged vegetables until just tender and drain. Cook the diced potatoes in the chicken broth until just tender, about 15 minutes. Do not let them get soft. Drain and cool. Mix together the green pepper, radishes, celery, scallions, water chestnuts, peas, and green beans. Season the vegetables with salt and garlic. In a flat casserole (10"x 14") place a layer of the potatoes, then a layer of the seasoned vegetable mixture, and keep alternating layers, ending with the potatoes.

Make the sauce by combining the mustard dressing, mayonnaise, sour cream, grated onion, dill, salt, pepper, and the French dressing, and blend all well. Adjust the seasoning to your own liking. Pour over the vegetable mixture and let stand in the refrigerator for a minimum of 5 hours or a maximum of 3 days. Do not freeze.

AVANT-GARDE VEGETABLES

Viva vegetarians! They may not convert you to their lifestyle, but they do dream up some satisfying combinations that turn meatless meals into a highly palatable pleasure. Lois Gould, author, avant-garde thinker, and Yoga classmate, makes this versatile, hot vegetable mélange for her family.

Because it requires minimal cooking time and is light and nourishing, I think it's perfect summer fare. The choice of four vegetables is easily made when the summer crop is abundant. You can also toss in any small amounts of vegetables that have accumulated in the refrigerator. There's no peeling or paring needed for most of them—just an easy, breezy affair to enjoy like a Gould novel. Serves 6.

6 cups of any 4 firm vegetables, cleaned, unpeeled, and cut into equal sized chunks (broccoli, carrots, cauliflower, celery, eggplant, mushrooms, onions, string beans, or zucchini)
Sea salt

2 cloves garlic, minced
Ground black pepper
3 tablespoons butter
1 can (10 ounces) Cheddar cheese soup
¼ cup fresh bread crumbs
½ cup fresh Cheddar cheese, grated

HOW TO: Place the vegetables in a steamer over hot water and cook until just fork tender; they should be undercooked. Drain and transfer to an oven-to-table shallow serving dish. Sprinkle with the salt, garlic, freshly ground pepper, and add the butter. Stir in the soup and blend all together. Cook for 5 minutes over moderate heat. Just before serving time, top with bread crumbs and fresh Cheddar cheese and pop into a moderate oven for 5 minutes until cheese melts. Serve immediately.

STEAK TARTARE

This is a robust dish that most people scrupulously avoid in restaurants, where freshness isn't always guaranteed. But at home, it's another matter. Consider it next time you are looking for a special hors d'oeuvre or a cookless main course. High protein and low carbohydrate eaters will appreciate this. Don't cut corners on the meat—here's an instance where good relations with the butcher are important. Serves 6 as an entrée.

1 ½ pounds lean, fresh ground beef absolutely fat-free
3 egg yolks (raw)
2 tablespoons capers
2 tablespoons onion, finely chopped
2 tablespoons parsley, finely chopped

6 anchovy fillets
Black pepper, freshly ground, to taste
Bunch of watercress
Lemon wedges
2 eggs, hard-boiled and chopped
Thinly sliced black bread

HOW TO: Place the meat in a wooden bowl and add the raw egg yolks, capers, onion, parsley, and anchovy fillets. Sprinkle with a generous amount of freshly ground black pepper. Mound on a salad platter surrounded with watercress. Garnish with more anchovy fillets and lemon wedges, and sprinkle with the chopped eggs. Serve with thinly sliced black bread.

BARBECUED BUTTERFLIED LAMB

Many men enjoy wearing the chef's toque blanche *and presiding over a grill. If you have that sort of help at hand and are looking for a change from the conventional spareribs, try this fuss-free barbecued lamb. The marinade comes from the outdoor party repertoire of Jane Holstein of Cazenovia, New York.*

Ask the butcher to bone a leg of lamb and remove every bit of fat surrounding the meat.

Accompany with plain or curry flavored white rice (See page 93.) and a vegetable salad. Serves 10.

7-pound leg of lamb, boned and trimmed of all fat
½ cup soy sauce
1 cup water

½ teaspoon powdered thyme
¼ teaspoon ground cardamon
3 cloves garlic, crushed

HOW TO: Mix together the soy sauce, water, herbs, and spices, and pour over the meat. Use a glass or ceramic dish, not a metal one. Marinate for at least 3 hours in the refrigerator. Start the charcoal fire about 2 hours before serving time. When the ashes are white, place the lamb flat on the grill, about 4 inches above the ashes. Roast for 45 minutes, turning once, until medium-well done. Place on a wooden board to carve into 1-inch thick slices.

SUGGESTED WINE: VILLA ANTINORI (CHIANTI CLASSICO, ITALY)

Thyme

GRILLED CHICKEN ALFRESCO

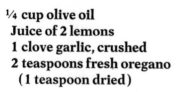

A tasty method of grilling chicken outdoors was found in A Traveler in Southern Italy *by H. V. Morton, a lively account of the author's adventures. I adapted the recipe below from a dish he described with gusto.*

The marinade flavors the chicken with pungent herbs, and the charcoal broiling on an outdoor grill of your preference brings out the succulence. Serves 4.

¼ cup olive oil
Juice of 2 lemons
1 clove garlic, crushed
2 teaspoons fresh oregano
  (1 teaspoon dried)

2 teaspoons parsley, chopped
Salt and pepper
2 broilers, split

HOW TO: Make a marinade of the olive oil, lemon juice, garlic, herbs, and seasonings. Set the broilers in a shallow dish and coat with the marinade. Allow to stand for at least 1 hour or longer before broiling on an outdoor charcoal grill. Remove the chickens from the marinade and cook over hot coals. Brush on additional marinade once or twice during the cooking process. Chickens should be done in about 45 minutes. Cut into serving pieces and eat picnic style.

SUGGESTED WINE: GRAVES SEC (DRY WHITE BORDEAUX) OR SAUVIGNON BLANC (CALIFORNIA)

TORTONI

When it comes to desserts, the Italians have fewer choices than some other peoples. But with superb dolces *like zabaglione and tortoni, who needs more? The tortoni turns up regularly on restaurant menus but it can be made easily and more deliciously at home. It's a form of Italian ice cream with an almond flavor and is prepared without cooking in individual fluted paper containers. To be sure the cups keep their shape while freezing, set them in muffin tins. You will have no serving dishes to clean up, a plus in hot weather.*

The original recipe appeared in a P.T.A. cookbook, which has long ago disappeared, but the memorable recipe lingers on. Makes 4 tortoni.

1 egg white	1 cup heavy cream
1 scant teaspoon dry instant coffee	1 teaspoon vanilla extract
⅛ teaspoon salt	⅛ teaspoon almond extract
¼ cup plus 2 tablespoons sugar	¼ cup almonds, finely ground

HOW TO: Beat the egg whites with the instant coffee and salt until meringue is stiff, but not dry. Gradually beat in the 2 tablespoons of sugar. Separately, whip the cream with the ¼ cup of sugar until stiff. Add the vanilla and almond flavorings to the cream mixture and then stir into the meringue mixture. Pour into fluted paper containers. Sprinkle with the ground almonds. Place in the freezer for several hours.

CRÈME DE MENTHE PIE—NO BAKE

Mint is a perennial cooler—now you can have it in an easy-to-make, no-bake pie. The only heat required is a few minutes on the stove to melt the chocolate. The rest can be assembled in about 10 minutes. This chocolate-mint flavoring is especially pleasant after grilled barbecued chicken or lamb. Prepare in the morning and refrigerate, dressing it up with sweetened whipped cream (or Cool Whip for slimmers) just before serving. Serves 6 generously.

¼ pound (1 stick) butter	3 tablespoons crème de menthe
1 cup confectioners' sugar	1 9-inch ready-made graham
2 ounces semisweet chocolate	cracker crust
2 eggs, well beaten	½ pint heavy cream whipped
1 teaspoon vanilla	with sugar added

HOW TO: Cream together the butter and sugar. Melt the chocolate over hot water and add to the butter and sugar mixture. Add the eggs and continue to beat until fluffy. Add the vanilla extract and crème de menthe. Pour mixture into unbaked pie shell. Refrigerate for several hours. Add the whipped cream topping at serving time.

110

8

Be An Artful Dodger

TRAVEL LIGHT

When you get the urge to view foreign lands,
You can travel light and use only your hands.
Look for adventure in the food that you choose
For a journey to Lebanon, make Baba Gannoujh.

Try Osso Buco when you can't make it to Rome,
Or eat bread as in Paris, but bake it at home.
Lunch on fine Oxtail as the English in Bath may,
Or munch on Baklava down a Yugoslav pathway.

EGGPLANT BABA GHANNOUJH
(Lebanon)

Plan a trip to the Middle East—with a cookbook. You run no risk of cancellation due to "political unrest." This appetizer is smooth enough to use as a dip with assorted crudités or you can serve it with pieces of soft flat Pita or Syrian bread, now stocked in the bread sections of many American supermarkets. Baba means "grandfather," and ghannoujh is defined as "soft food"; the combination translates as "soft food for a toothless old man." It is a light, creamy-colored delight for all ages. Makes 2 cups.

1 large eggplant
4 cloves garlic
1 teaspoon salt
¼ cup lemon juice

¼ cup sesame oil
Salt to taste
Parsley sprigs

HOW TO: Preheat oven to 350° F. Cut the eggplant into half, lengthwise. Broil, skin side up, until skin is black and crackling, about ½ hour. Peel off the skin, discard the liquid, and put the pulp into a blender. Pound the garlic with 1 teaspoon of salt. Mix smooth with 1 teaspoon of lemon juice and add to the eggplant pulp. Mix the remaining lemon juice and oil, alternating small quantities to insure smooth blending. Season with salt. Pour into a serving dish and chill. When ready to serve, garnish with parsley sprigs. Serve with whole, soft, round flat bread to be broken into small pieces as needed.

POTATO BLINI IN A BLENDER
(Russia)

Russian style pancakes which use potatoes instead of buckwheat flour are a favorite of Andrei Sedych, editor-in-chief of Novoye Russkoye Slovo *(the oldest Russian-language daily newspaper published in America). He and his wife Jenny Grey, a singer, frequently entertain leading Russian artists at their home in New York City.*

Goodbye to the nuisance of potato and onion scraping—the blender whips this up in minutes for quick serving after a concert or light meal any time of day. Dress it with red or black caviar and a dollop of sour cream to revive memories of an evening at the Bolshoi. Makes 12 blini.

2 eggs	**¼ cup flour**
1 small onion, chopped	**Vegetable oil**
1 teaspoon salt	**½ pint sour cream**
2 cups raw potatoes, peeled, diced	**2 ounces red or black caviar**

HOW TO: Break the eggs into a blender. Add the onion, salt, and half the potatoes. Cover and turn the blender on high for 1 minute. Uncover and add the flour and remaining potatoes. Give the blender another whirl for a minute. Pour the batter into a pitcher and let stand in the refrigerator until it chills a bit.

Pour about 2 tablespoons of batter for each pancake onto a lightly greased hot griddle and cook on both sides until brown. Serve with sour cream and caviar in separate bowls.

113

CUCUMBERS BORANI
(Turkey)

People who live in sweltering climates usually have an interesting array of heat-beaters. I found this Near Eastern dish a refreshing appetizer, as well as the perfect condiment with a barbecued leg of lamb.

In Istanbul one of the popular restaurants in the center of town displays a tasty array of dishes in semi-cafeteria style; one selects one's food at a glass covered counter, and a waiter brings it to your table. Following my third portion of Cucumbers Borani, our guide noticed that I was becoming addicted. He obtained the recipe and presented it as a surprise when he returned us to our hotel. Serves 4.

2 cartons (8 ounces each) plain yogurt
1 large cucumber, peeled and chopped
1 tablespoon onion, minced, or
1 small clove garlic, minced
3 tablespoons mint leaves, finely chopped (about 6 sprigs), or 2 teaspoons, dried

½ teaspoon lemon juice or white wine vinegar
3 tablespoons walnuts, chopped
3 tablespoons golden raisins
¼ teaspoon majoram and sweet basil
Salt and pepper to taste

HOW TO: Beat the yogurt until smooth and stir in all the remaining ingredients. Season with salt and pepper. Keep chilled and serve in a cool bowl. If you serve it as an appetizer, have some unsalted crackers to go with it.

Basil

PESTO GENOVESE
(Italy)

Pesto is a traditional sauce thought to have been devised by the cooks of Genoa even before the Renaissance. It's name translates as "paste," and there are many versions of it, but the two fundamental ingredients are fresh basil and garlic. Frequently used on pasta, fish, or meats—it is really good on everything.

Pesto may be kept indefinitely and spooned directly from the jar onto hot food or into a sauce. Use about ½ cup of pesto or less, diluted with 2 tablespoons of warm water, for each pound of freshly cooked pasta. Toss quickly and serve immediately on hot plates.

Some purists make pesto with a mortar and pestle, working the dry ingredients into a paste and thus wedding the flavors before adding the olive oil. The result is a loose, rough-textured pesto. The blender-made variation below was discovered in the delightful book, Italian Family Cooking *by Edward Giobbi, the well-known artist, fellow epicure, and country neighbor. It's the best of its kind I have ever tasted. Yields about 2 cups.*

5 cups fresh basil leaves, washed, drained, and tightly packed
¼ cup parsley, Italian if possible, chopped
¾ cup olive oil

2 tablespoons garlic, finely minced
½ cup pignoli nuts (pine nuts)
1 teaspoon salt
½ cup Romano or Parmesan cheese

HOW TO: Put all the ingredients into the container of an electric blender and blend, scraping down with a rubber spatula as necessary, until a smooth paste forms. If the pesto is not to be used immediately, spoon it into a glass jar or a plastic container and cover with ¾ inch of olive oil. Cover tightly and store in the refrigerator or in a cool place. Can be kept almost indefinitely as long as it's covered with the oil.

NO-KNEAD FRENCH BREAD
(France)

You may not be a bread baker, but this recipe is sure to break down your resistance. It comes from well-traveled Florence Green of New York City and Kent Cliffs, New York, who learned to make it, curiously enough, in San Miguel de Allende, Mexico. This is the nearest thing I have found to a French baguette, those wonderful long thin breads we buy fresh from the boulangerie whenever we picnic in France. Such a bread must have been the inspiration for Omar Khayyam's famous line, "A Jug of Wine, a Loaf of Bread—and Thou."

You will find the process uncomplicated, the ingredients simple; but I caution you to follow the recipe exactly as written. No short cuts please. What makes this bread fun for me is the fact that it requires ABSOLUTELY NO KNEADING OF DOUGH. The yeast does all the work for you! It's lovely to look at, to bake, to freeze, to reheat in minutes, and to have on hand for flabbergasted guests.

You do not have to tend to it the whole time, but don't get too far away—a fine indoor activity on a rainy day. It takes about 3½ hours from start to finish with just an occasional visit to the kitchen to shape and bake. You will need a large flat cookie sheet and a 4-quart mixing bowl. (See color photograph on page 78.) Yields 2 loaves 18 inches long.

1 package (¼ ounce) active dry yeast dissolved in	½ cup milk
¼ cup warm water	2 tablespoons butter
4 cups unbleached flour	1 cup warm water
2 teaspoons salt	1 egg white, lightly beaten with
2 tablespoons sugar	1 tablespoon cold water

HOW TO: Dissolve the yeast in ¼ cup warm water or as per instructions on the yeast package. Let stand at least 10 minutes. Sift together all the dry ingredients (flour, salt, and sugar), and place in a large bowl. Scald the milk in a small saucepan, but do not boil. Add the butter, remove from heat and add the yeast, stirring to dissolve any lumps. Add the warm water. Pour the liquid mix into the dry ingredients. DO NOT BEAT. Just fold in the dry ingredients until all have been absorbed into the liquid.

Butter a sheet of wax paper, place it buttered side down over the bowl. Cover the paper with a warm, wet dishtowel and place the bowl on the top rack in an UNLIT oven with a pan of hot water on the rack below (see drawing) for 1½ to 2 hours until the dough has doubled in size.

Remove and place on a lightly floured counter or board. Lightly flour hands. Divide the dough. Pat each half into a rectangular shape (6″ x 8″ x ¼″). Pick up the ends and fold toward you into 3 layers. Narrow the ends into loaf points. Place each loaf diagonally on a lightly buttered cookie sheet. With a knife make 3 or 4 slashes about ¾ way through the dough. Cover the shaped dough again with the buttered wax paper and the warm, wet dishtowel. Refill the water pan with hot water and leave in the oven. Replace in the UNLIT oven for another 20 minutes to rise again. Remove the dough from the oven, discard the wax paper, and remove the dishtowel.

Preheat oven to 400° F. Refill the water pan with hot water and leave in the oven. Bake loaves for 15 minutes. Then lower flame to 375° F. for 15 minutes. Spread the tops with lightly beaten egg white to glaze. Continue baking for another 10 to 15 minutes until top crust is lightly browned. Total baking time is about 45 minutes.

The bread, wrapped in plastic wrap or aluminum foil, can be frozen while still hot, to be reheated when needed.

For those who want a more authentic looking French loaf, here is a place to order French bread pans as pictured: Write to ParisX, 500 Independence Avenue, S.E., Washington, D.C. 20003 for their catalog.

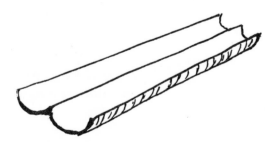

ARTICHOKES BUCA LAPI
(Italy)

The Buca Lapi is one of the oldest and most celebrated restaurants in Florence, where Florentines and foreigners are frequently willing to wait in line out on the street just for the privilege of dining there.

Gino, the head chef at the Buca Lapi, gave me the recipe for the remarkable vegetable dish which follows. We sampled it during the great cooking festival, Cucina de Tuscana, a week-long celebration held every October, in which local restaurants vie with one another to prepare specialties of the Tuscan region. Serves 3.

**6 small or medium-sized
  artichokes
½ cup flour
1 slice bacon**

**1 tablespoon olive oil
2 tablespoons consommé
  or water
Pepper**

HOW TO: Cut off the stalks of the artichokes and remove any tough outer leaves. Slice off the tops of the artichokes to remove the tips. Wash thoroughly and roll lightly in the flour. Cut the bacon into little pieces and in a heavy skillet sauté in olive oil until browned. Put in the artichokes and cook for 10 minutes. Add the water or consommé, cover the pan, and continue cooking over low heat for another 15 minutes, or until tender. Season with a little pepper before serving.

OSSO BUCCO
(Italy)

The North Italians make an elegant form of stew which they call Osso Buco after the marrow-filled veal shank bones which are its chief ingredient. This particular version is my own, adapted over the years from several sources, none of which I can now remember. In fact, I had forgotten my own, too. Fortunately, a friend has proved better organized than I, and I am grateful to Ruth Kaplan of New York City for reminding me of this neglected delight and returning it to my repertoire. Serves 4 to 6.

2 tablespoons olive oil
2 small carrots, diced
2 small celery stalks, diced
1 onion, minced
4 to 6 pieces of veal shanks,
   cut in 3-inch lengths
Salt and pepper to taste

½ teaspoon fines herbes
   (Spice Islands brand)
1 cup tomato sauce
½ cup dry white wine
½ cup chicken broth
Bay leaf
Slivered rind of 1 lemon

HOW TO: Place the olive oil in a Dutch oven and brown the carrots, celery, and onion over low heat. Then add the meat. Brown well over high heat, turning frequently until the vegetables and meat are well browned. Add the salt, pepper, and fines herbes. Add the tomato sauce, white wine, chicken broth, bay leaf, and lemon rind. Bring to a boil. Then lower the heat and simmer in a covered pot for 1 ½ hours until the meat is tender. Remove the lemon rinds before serving.

SUGGESTED WINE: BEAUJOLAIS BLANC (WHITE BURGUNDY) OR EMERALD RIESLING (CALIFORNIA)

INTOXICATED ROAST PORK
(Italy)

How can you resist trying to make an intoxicated roast pork? The title is irresistible, and so is this Italian dish. The pork will be thoroughly cooked, but will retain its beautiful flavored juices and eliminate most of the fat. The choice of the size of the roast loin of pork is yours, depending on the number of people you plan to feed, but the remainder of the ingredients do not vary. An 8-ribbed loin serves 4 to 6.

4-to-5-pound loin of pork
1 clove of garlic
3 whole cloves
4 or 5 leaves fresh sage or
   ½ teaspoon dried
3 or 4 sprigs fresh rosemary or
   ½ teaspoon dried

3 or 4 leaves fresh basil or
   ½ teaspoon dried
Salt
Pepper
1 cup dry white wine
1 cup tomato sauce

HOW TO: Preheat oven to 425°F. For this you will need a roasting pan with a rack and a cover. Have the butcher saw through the rib bones of the loin to partially separate the chops. Place the pork, skin side up, on a rack in the

119

roasting pan. Bake, uncovered, for 20 minutes to brown the surface. Remove the roast from the rack and skim the fat from the pan. Remove the rack and return the roast to the pan. Season the meat with garlic, cloves, sage, rosemary, basil, salt, and pepper. Add the wine. Lower heat to 300°F. and continue cooking the pork until the wine is reduced by half, approximately 20 minutes. Stir the tomato sauce into the remaining juices. Cover the roast and cook for about 2 hours, adding a little hot water if the sauce becomes too thick. Remove the roast to a hot platter to carve. Pour off the sauce, skim off fat, and serve fat-free sauce over the meat.

SUGGESTED WINE: BROUILLY (FRUITY RED BURGUNDY) OR VINHO VERDE (RED PORTUGUESE)

PULE ME HARR
(Albania)

If our mythical Albanian peasant got carried away during his foray into the barnyard and made off with not only 2 eggs but also the chicken, he would surely cook pule *("chicken")* me harr *("walnut"), for such is the stuff of ecstasy in Albania. Walnuts, of course, is the ingredient that gives this culinary trip its exoticism. The recipe comes from* The Cookbook of the United Nations. *Serves 6.*

3½- to 5-pound stewing chicken
1 teaspoon salt
½ teaspoon black pepper
3 cups water

1 pound shelled walnuts
  (2 cups)
4 tablespoons butter
2 tablespoons flour
1 clove garlic

HOW TO: Preheat oven to 325° F. Season the chicken with salt and pepper. Place in a large baking dish, add the water, cover, and cook for 2 hours, or until the chicken is tender. When the chicken is done, remove and cut into serving pieces. Save the broth. Crush the walnuts in a blender or with a rolling pin. Melt the butter in a skillet large enough to hold the chicken parts, which will be added later; add the flour, stirring until brown. Gradually add the crushed walnuts, garlic, and chicken broth to the browned flour mixture. Blend together. Add the chicken to the sauce, coating each piece. Continue cooking the chicken over low heat until sauce is thick. Remove from heat, cover, and let stand for 5 to 10 minutes before serving.

SUGGESTED WINE: MACON BLANC (FRESH DRY WHITE BURGUNDY) OR NEW YORK CHABLIS

CHICKEN WITH WHITE PORT
& GROUND CORIANDER
(Portugal)

A visit to Portugal in early springtime is a feast for the eyes and the palate. From Lisbon, its capital, one can travel a short distance in any direction to find gastronomic specialties.

The beach resorts along Portugal's southern coast are still unspoiled. One of their great attractions is the surrounding groves of blossoming almond and fig trees laden with fruit which, as one native proudly explained, supply American companies with "figgies for Newtons."

I was attracted to this recipe in Cooking in a Casserole *by Robert C. Ackart who says this dish should be served with a bowl of rice prepared with a bit of saffron and tomato. Serves 6, can be doubled.*

2 3½-pound chickens or 12 chicken parts cut into serving pieces enough for 6 persons
4 tablespoons butter
2 tablespoons flour
3 garlic cloves, split
½ teaspoons white pepper

1½ teaspoons ground coriander
1½ cups white port wine
Hot water
1 cup heavy cream or half-and-half
2 tablespoons parsley, finely chopped

HOW TO: In a 6-quart casserole melt the butter and brown the chicken all over. Remove the chicken and set aside. Mix the flour with the pan juices. Add the garlic and seasonings and blend. Return the chicken to the pan. Add the wine and enough water to cover. Bring to a boil, then reduce heat, cover, and simmer for 40 minutes, or until tender. Just before serving remove the chicken pieces to a warm dish. Further reduce the liquid in the casserole to about 1¼ cups. Stir in the cream and simmer for 3 minutes. Place the chicken on a serving dish and cover with sauce. Sprinkle with chopped parsley.

SUGGESTED WINE: BEREICH BERNKASTELER (SEMIDRY MOSELLE)

A RARE DELICACY

What can you tell a seven-year-old son about an adult's trip to Europe? Perhaps a bit about castles and kings? There was little, I felt, that would interest my little boy, or that he could visualize with his limited experience.

But wait, perhaps, one subject might work for a few minutes—FOOD! "You'll never guess what strange foods they serve in foreign countries!" I began. "I ate frog's legs and snails in France. In Italy I tasted pig's feet and a small fish from the sea called squid—it has little tentacles like a tiny octopus."

I raised my arms, extended both hands, and spread my fingers wide, to create a more vivid image. I had no idea whether my colorful account had left much of an impression, although Paul seemed attentive at the moment.

One afternoon, a few days later, I was pleased to overhear him recounting to a school playmate in his own way all that I had described.

"Ya know, my mother just came back from Europe and she ate the craziest food there. She went to France and she ate frog's legs—yccch! and snails —ick! and in Italy she ate pig's feet—and something called squid—that's the testicles of an octopus, ya know."

Oxtails may be equally curious to some. I found an unusual recipe for oxtails at a world-renowned 3-star restaurant, The Hole in the Wall, in Bath, an English city famous for its Regency architecture and Roman baths.

OXTAILS WITH GRAPES
(England)

Whenever I want to recapture my trip to Bath, I cook this dish. It is presented here exactly the way Heather Crosby, owner and partner with Perry Smith of The Hole in the Wall restaurant, copied it from her recipe file when I asked if I might include it in this book. I have since made it numerous times with unfailing success.

For those unfamiliar with the tail of the beef, it's worth noting that the meat is very tender: "The nearer the bone—the sweeter the meat" is an old country saying. The grape pits add crunch for surprise and piquancy. Prepare for cooking in a brief 15 minutes and slow cook for 3 hours a day ahead of time or in the early morning for the same evening. Oxtails are modestly priced and come ready-cut in the meat department Serves 6.

2 oxtails, ready-cut
½ pound fatty bacon, cut into
   1-inch pieces
4 large onions, quartered and cut
   into 1-inch chunks
8 large carrots, sliced into ½-inch
   rounds

4 cloves garlic, sliced
¼ teaspoon powdered thyme
3 bay leaves
6 parsley sprigs
2 pounds green grapes with seeds
½ teaspoon powdered mace
Salt and pepper to taste

HOW TO: Preheat oven to 200° F. Remove all the fat and gristle from the oxtail pieces. This is easier to do if the meat has been partially frozen first and the fat is firm. In a large heavy Dutch oven melt the diced bacon. Add the onions, carrots, garlic, thyme, bay leaves, and parsley. Fry all the vegetables thoroughly over medium heat. Season the oxtails well with salt and pepper. Add the seasoned oxtails to the Dutch oven and cook all together until the meat is a bit brown. Skim off the excess fat, if any, from the top. Add 1½ pounds of green grapes (unstemmed)—juice, pits, and all—squeezing with hands. Add the mace. Cover and cook in a very slow oven for 3 hours. When the meat is quite tender remove from the oven. Place the oxtail pieces in a stove-to-table serving dish to keep warm. Thoroughly mash the sauce, but do not purée. Check the seasoning to your taste, then pour the sauce over the meat. Garnish with the remaining ½ pound of whole green grapes before serving.

SUGGESTED WINE: BAROLO (ITALIAN RED) OR ZINFANDEL (CALIFORNIA)

EPICURE'S GÚLYÁS
(Hungary)

This Hungarian dish is a splendid way of serving beef steak and green peppers. It is perfectly suited to an inexpensive yet tender cut of meat, and requires no slicing at serving time. Dieters will like it because the meat has been trimmed of all fat, and you will like it because it can be made early in the day and reheated at serving time.

This dish comes from a Hungarian with epicure tastes, the late Joseph Douglas Weiss, a noted architect. His wife Jean of Chappaqua, New York, gifted me with the secrets of this family treasure. Serve it for a dinner-long stopover in Budapest. Serves 4.

6 or 8 slices (¼-inch thick) of shoulder-cut beef called "chicken steak"
Flour
Salt and pepper to taste
2 tablespoons butter
2 large onions, sliced or chopped

2 cans (10 ounces) whole tomatoes
1 large green pepper, seeded and sliced in strips
1 teaspoon paprika
1 tablespoon parsley, chopped

HOW TO: Sprinkle the meat lightly with flour that has been seasoned with salt and pepper. Place the meat slices in a stove-to-table shallow pan with 2 tablespoons of butter and heat until lightly browned. Add the onions, tomatoes, green pepper, and paprika. Simmer, covered, for 1 hour over low heat. When the meat is tender, remove it with a slotted spoon and set it aside. Put the vegetables through a strainer. Return the meat slices to the serving pan and pour the puréed sauce over the meat. Let stand or reheat as necessary. Sprinkle with a bit of chopped parsley before serving.

SUGGESTED WINE: CÔTES DE BOURG (SOLID RED BORDEAUX) OR BARBERA (CALIFORNIA)

BOEUF D'AUTUN
(France)

Beef prices being what they are, when I make a beef dish using a good cut I want to be sure the quality of the meat is not lost under an avalanche of other ingredients and flavors. This French ragout seems to be just right. It has a superb sauce, well-laced with the red wine of Burgundy, a splash of brandy, and a good pour of Madeira; but the meat is still the star performer. The original inspiration comes from Autun, a small Burgundian city noted for its fine twelfth-century Romanesque cathedral of St. Lazare.

Instead of wrapping the bouquet garni in cheesecloth, as the French do, I season with the Spice Islands' brand of bouquet-garni, a fuss-free blend that gives the same flavor. Here is the recipe, with my own measurements translated from the French into Amerenglish. It is delicious atop buttered white rice. Serves 4.

2 pounds good lean beef for
   stewing, cut into 1½-inch cubes
3 tablespoons butter
1 tablespoon flour
Salt and pepper to taste
1½ cups red wine (a good
   Burgundy preferred here)
2 onions, coarsely chopped
1 clove garlic, finely chopped

2 shallots, finely chopped
1 carrot, cut into ¼-inch rounds
1 tablespoon Spice Islands'
   bouquet-garni or fines herbes
1 veal knuckle bone, cracked
   (if available)
1 tablespoon brandy
4 tablespoons Madeira wine
½ pound mushroom caps

HOW TO: In a heavy Dutch oven or casserole brown the beef in 2 tablespoons of butter. Sprinkle the meat with the flour and blend thoroughly with the butter. Add the salt, pepper and wine. Keep warm over low heat.

In a small frying pan sauté the onions in the remaining butter until

lightly browned and soft. Add to the meat, together with the garlic, shallots, and carrot slices. Season with bouquet-garni. Add the veal knuckle and enough water to cover. Simmer, covered, over low heat for 3½ hours, or until meat is very tender and the sauce is a rich, dark brown.

Half an hour before serving remove veal bone, add the brandy and the Madeira as well as the mushroom caps and warm gently.

SUGGESTED WINE: POMMARD (FULL RED BURGUNDY)..

RAGOUT IN THE MANNER OF OSTIA
(Italy)

For archeology buffs who will enjoy a trip back to pre-Christian times, this dish comes down to us unchanged from the ancient Etruscan city of Ostia, just a short distance from the Da Vinci airport in Rome.

I dug this artifact out of Horizon *Magazine from a story about Etruscan life. The seasonings are pungent and gutsy enough to "stick to the ribs." It should be served with medium-sized noodles, either green or white, with a bit of butter and grated Parmesan cheese, or with large-kernel Italian rice (Avorio is my favorite brand). Sprinkle the top with plenty of chopped parsley. This is an overnight affair, so allow enough time. Serves 6.*

2 tablespoons cracked black peppercorns
½ teaspoon dill weed
½ teaspoon powdered cumin
1 bay leaf, crushed
1 teaspoon salt
2 pounds beef, top sirloin or equivalent, cut into slices (3"x ½")

2 cups dry red wine
1 tablespoon honey
4 tablespoons olive oil
3 tablespoons butter
2 leeks, chopped (bulbs only)
1 onion, diced
2 teaspoons cornstarch

HOW TO: Mix the peppercorns, dill, cumin, and bay leaf with 1 teaspoon of salt. Wipe the meat dry and then press seasonings into the meat—all over. Place in a flat glass or enamel pan so that meat pieces are touching each other. Pour in the wine, which has been mixed with the honey, and 2 tablespoons of olive oil, and marinate overnight.

The next morning remove the meat from marinade with a slotted spoon. Gently pat the meat dry with a paper towel. Set the marinade aside and reserve. Melt the butter and the remaining 2 tablespoons of olive oil in a heavy casserole with a lid. Brown the meat on one side—turn—and then add the leeks and onion. When well browned all over, add the marinade and just enough water to cover. Bring to a boil, cover, lower the heat and simmer for 2 hours, or until meat is tender. Dilute the cornstarch with a little water and add to the stew. Stir and simmer until thickened. Correct seasoning. Serve on a warmed serving platter.

SUGGESTED WINE: NUITS ST. GEORGE (FULL RED BURGUNDY)

DAINTY DANISH CRESCENTS
(Denmark)

This recipe is a Danish transplant that thrives in Scarsdale, New York, where it is served by the P.T.A. mothers with coffee. They (the crescents) disappear in seconds. The dough must be refrigerated overnight before baking. It is a nice item to have on hand as accompaniment to a coffee break or a brown-bag lunch. Makes 24 crescents.

¼ **pound (1 stick) sweet butter**
1 **package (4 ounces) cream cheese**
1 **cup flour**
1 **tablespoon ground cinnamon**

¼ **cup sugar**
¼ **cup walnuts, finely chopped**
2 **tablespoons strawberry or raspberry jam**

HOW TO: Mix together the butter, cream cheese, and flour. This is great fun to do by hand. Make a ball and refrigerate overnight wrapped in a piece of wax paper or Saran wrap. When ready to bake, preheat oven to 350° F. Divide the ball of dough. Lightly flour a board or counter and a rolling pin. Take half of the dough and roll out as thin as possible, about ¼ inch thick,

127

into a roughly square or rectangular shape. Mix together the cinnamon, sugar, and chopped walnuts, and sprinkle the mixture over rolled-out dough. Then cut the dough into small 2-inch base triangles, and place a bit of jelly in each center. Roll up each triangle, starting from the base and rolling to the tip. Lightly grease a cookie sheet. Bend the ends of each rolled-up triangle so that it is crescent-shaped. Place crescents on the cookie sheet and bake for 15 minutes or until golden.

BAKLAVA
(Yugoslavia)

This internationally known dessert is well-liked in Yugoslavia, where it varies slightly from one household to another. Fortunately, the phyllo pastry, which is the essential ingredient, is now available at specialty food stores handling Greek and Middle Eastern groceries. I tasted this in Dubrovnik, the famed beach resort in Yugoslavia, and I am happy to be able to make it so effortlessly in my own kitchen. (See color photograph on page 79.) Yields 20 pieces.

1 pound phyllo dough sheets
½ pound (approximately) butter, melted
1 pound walnuts, shelled and ground

½ cup almonds, blanched and ground
2 cups sugar
2 teaspoons cinnamon
1½ cups water
3 tablespoons lemon juice

HOW TO: Preheat oven to 350° F. Arrange a third of the pastry sheets, each brushed with melted butter, in a flat baking dish (10"x 14"). Combine the nuts, half cup of sugar, and cinnamon. Sprinkle half of this mixture over the phyllo sheets. Place another third of the pastry sheets, each sheet brushed with melted butter, over the nut mixture. Repeat with another layer of the nut mixture and cover with the remaining buttered third of the pastry sheets. With a sharp knife cut into diamond-shaped pieces. Bake for 1 hour, or until cooked. Remove from the oven and cool a little. Meanwhile, in a saucepan, combine the remaining 1½ cups of sugar, water, and lemon juice. Bring to a boil. Lower heat and simmer until mixture thickens into a syrup. Pour, while still warm, over the baklava. Leave at room temperature until ready to serve.

Commit
A
Little Larceny

9

TURN DROSS INTO GOLD

Boil a Beef Tongue, to escape any traps,
Add a fine sauce made of crushed ginger-snaps.
Use handy ready-mades in clever disguise,
For the subtle delight of a Sole Surprise.

The Raspberry Fooler's a sight to behold,
With sleight of hand you turn dross into gold.
Add magical moisture with some apricot fakery,
For a better cake than you'll find in a bakery.

SAVORY SPARKLERS

Sesame seeds add sparkle to hot hors d'oeuvres. These were introduced to me by Julie Levinson of Teaneck, New Jersey, at a cocktail party. Julie used a crabmeat filling, and wonderful it was, but for variety at a fraction of the price, I devised two alternative easy-to-make fillings of spinach and mushrooms using the same basic technique. Because this hot appetizer may be made a day or two in advance and should be frozen before heating, you can serve as many as you like to suit your needs. The remainder can be set aside to use for an unexpected occasion. A few minutes under the broiler readies them for serving. Yields 60 pieces.

20 slices soft white bread
 1 package (8 ounces) Velveeta
   cheese or
 1 jar (8 ounces) Cheez-Wiz
 ½ pound (2 sticks) butter

1 can (7½ ounces) crabmeat
2 cups sesame seeds
1 package (10 ounces) frozen
  chopped spinach
4 fresh mushrooms, chopped fine

 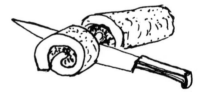

HOW TO: Prepare the bread slices by cutting off the crusts. Roll each piece with a rolling pin until thin. Set aside to be filled with the spreads. Melt the cheese with 1 stick of butter in the top of a double boiler. The butter and cheese may separate, but that's alright. Let cool. Pick the crabmeat clean, remove any shell. Add the crabmeat to the cheese mixture, stirring well until the mixture is spreadable. Spread a scant layer on one side of the bread and roll up. Melt the remaining 1 stick of butter and brush each crab roll with butter. Place the sesame seeds on a piece of aluminum foil and coat each roll with the seeds. Place the rolls, seam side down, in a flat pan that has been covered with aluminum foil or plastic wrap, and store in the freezer. When ready to serve, remove and cut each roll into thirds. Heat unthawed rolls in the broiler under low heat until the sesame seeds toast to a golden brown, about 3 or 4 minutes.

Cook the chopped spinach according to package directions. Sauté the chopped mushrooms very lightly in a little butter. Substitute the spinach or the mushrooms for the crabmeat and follow the rest of the recipe as given above. Arrange on a serving platter.

SPICY COCKTAIL MEATBALLS

You'll love the grand-larcenous approach to creating this great crowd pleaser. The dish can be prepared days in advance, frozen, and served effortlessly in a chafing dish, leaving you free to swing at your own party. Yields 50 to 60 morsels.

1 jar (10 ounces) grape jelly
1 bottle (12 ounces) chili sauce
Juice of 1 lemon
2 pounds beef, ground round or
  chuck

1 egg, slightly beaten
1 large onion, grated
Salt to taste
4 tablespoons butter

HOW TO: In a saucepan mix and heat the grape jelly, chili sauce, and lemon juice. Meanwhile, combine the ground beef, egg, onion, and salt, and shape into meatballs about 1 inch in diameter. Sauté meatballs in butter over low heat until browned. Add the meatballs to the warm sauce and transfer to your fanciest chafing dish. Simmer over low heat. If you prefer to make this dish in advance, freeze the meat and sauce separately. Remove from the freezer a few hours before serving time and reheat together until thoroughly warmed. Don't forget cocktail picks.

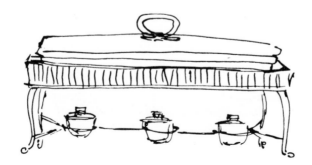

SEAFOOD KENNEDY

Here's a way to make you feel like a slim millionaire, just in case you aren't. Seafood Kennedy delights as a hot hors d'oeuvre or a main luncheon dish. Fresh or frozen crabmeat mixed with mayonnaise plus the Worcestershire sauce and potato chips makes this look and taste grand luxe indeed.

Seafood Kennedy is a fine substitute for a quiche—and the simple preparation involved makes it foolproof. Do the first steps early in the morning and pop the mélange into the oven for baking a half hour before serving time. Serves 6 to 8.

1 pound fresh crabmeat or 3 packages (6 ounces each) frozen	1 tablespoon Worcestershire sauce
1 pound small shrimp, boiled, shelled, and deveined	½ teaspoon salt
1½ cups celery, finely chopped	1 cup prepared mayonnaise
¼ cup onion, finely chopped	2 cups crushed potato chips
	Paprika

HOW TO: Pick the crabmeat clean and remove shell bits. Place all the ingredients, except the potato chips and paprika, in a flat oven-to-table casserole. Blend well. You can allow the mixture to stand in the refrigerator for several hours. About 40 minutes before you are ready to serve preheat oven to 400° F. Crush the potato chips and sprinkle on top with a dash of paprika over all. Bake in the oven for about 30 minutes or until crisp. Serve immediately.

SUGGESTED WINE: POUILLY FUMÉ (FRAGRANT WHITE LOIRE) OR FRASCATI (DRY WHITE ITALIAN)

FILLETS OF SOLE SURPRISE

Here's a fraudulently delicious fish entrée. The surprise is in its ease of preparation—possible because it uses ready-made cream of celery soup and ginger ale to effect the beautiful golden sauce. The fish is filled with shrimp and flavorful herbs. Evelyn Lauder offered this favorite of hers to me. Serve it on a bed of rice (see recipe on page 93) mixed with green peas. It's a beauty. Serves 4.

2 tablespoons butter
½ pound fresh shrimp, cleaned, cooked, and chopped
4 fresh fillets of sole (about 1½ pounds)
Onion powder to taste
Garlic powder to taste

1 teaspoon dill weed
1 tablespoon bouquet garni (Spice Islands brand)
½ teaspoon fennel seeds
1 can cream of celery soup (Campbell's)
1 bottle (7 ounces) ginger ale

HOW TO: Preheat oven to 300° F. Rub the butter on the bottom and the sides of a pyrex baking dish large enough to hold the 4 fillets when rolled and leave space in between for sauce. Take each fillet and lay flat on a piece of wax paper, with inside surface on top (outside surface is smoother). Sprinkle some onion and garlic powders, dill weed, bouquet garni, and a few fennel seeds on each fillet. Then place a tablespoon of chopped shrimp on the center of the fish. Top with a tablespoon of the celery soup. Add a few additional sprinkles of bouquet garni, dill weed, and fennel seeds. Roll up each fillet and place in the dish. Add a little more seasonings to the shrimp. Spoon the remaining soup over the top of each fillet. Now slowly drizzle the ginger ale over all, distributing it evenly. Place the dish into the oven and allow the liquid to reduce and thicken until golden. This takes about 1 hour.

SUGGESTED WINE: SOAVE (ITALIAN WHITE)

SNAPPY TONGUE IN GINGER SAUCE

Sliced, cooked tongue deserves more friends than it has. Dressed-up with a sweet and sour sauce, it makes a memorable first impression on newcomers and wins over anyone who snubbed it earlier. Both the tongue and sauce may be prepared a day or two in advance and stored in the refrigerator. The sauce part of the recipe yields about 1 cup, enough for a 4- or 5-pound tongue, which will serve 8 people. If you prefer to serve the tongue without sauce—say, sliced cold, for lunch— it will probably take care of 12.

4 or 5 pounds smoked beef tongue
6 ginger snaps
1 cup boiling water
½ cup brown sugar

⅛ cup white vinegar
1 lemon, sliced very thin
¼ cup raisins

HOW TO: Place the ready-smoked tongue in a large kettle and cover with water. No seasonings are necessary. Bring to a boil and simmer for 3 to 4 hours, depending on size of the tongue. Remove from the water and discard all but 2 cups of the liquid. Cut off the fatty end and remove the skin from the tongue. Slice the meat horizontally into ⅛-inch slices and arrange on a stove-to-table platter. If you do not plan to serve it immediately, leave the whole tongue in 2 cups of liquid and store in the refrigerator. Later it may be sliced and served cold or sliced and reheated gently in its own juice and drained.

Meanwhile, to make the sauce, crush the ginger snaps and put into boiling water until they dissolve. Add the brown sugar and vinegar, and stir well until the sauce is smooth. Add the lemon slices and raisins. Pour over the hot tongue or store it in the refrigerator until ready to use, at which time reheat the tongue and sauce together over low heat.

SUGGESTED WINE: WITH HOT TONGUE, BEAUNE (WARM RED BURGUNDY). WITH COLD TONGUE, BEER OR ALE

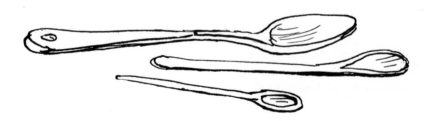

FOOLPROOF BAKED BRISKET

The cleanest, neatest way to insure perfect seasoning for a pot roast that I know of is one introduced to me by a neighbor Gladys Herring. My own addition is to insert slivers of garlic into the meat and brown it thoroughly before applying the onion soup mix. Place the whole concoction into a brown-in-oven bag or wrap it in aluminum foil. This avoids all clean-up before and after serving, which is good sense especially when entertaining. Pure gold. Serves 6.

**4 to 5 pounds first- or second-cut
  fresh brisket of beef
  (not corned)**

**2 cloves garlic, slivered
1 envelope Lipton's dried
  onion soup mix**

HOW TO: Preheat oven to 350° F. Make gashes in both sides of the meat and insert the garlic slivers. In a heavy saucepan on top of the stove brown the meat well to seal in all the juices and place on a large piece of aluminum foil or in a brown-in-oven bag. Cover the entire pot roast, both sides, with a package Lipton's dried onion soup mix—or any other dried brand. Seal the aluminum foil or the brown-in-oven bag (be sure to puncture holes in the bag as instructed to allow steam to escape). Roast for 3½ hours until tender. This combination of seasoning and juices are so perfect you need never worry about the flavors.

I often take the meat out and slice it thin across the grain, placing the slices and gravy in a flat oven-to-table dish to warm before serving.

SUGGESTED WINE: CÔTES DU RHONE (FRUITY RED RHONE) OR DÔLE (RED SWISS)

MOCK CHEESECAKE

Ralph Pomerance, the noted architect of New York City, remembers this favorite from his boyhood. It is made to order for those who enjoy a taste of lemon at the end of a meal. No cheese or sugar necessary and no dough to bake—just whipped up with a few flicks of the egg beater. Fun to make. Serves 6.

**6 eggs, separated
1 can sweetened condensed milk
Juice and grated rind of 2 lemons
½ teaspoon cream or tartar**

**Pinch of salt
10 graham crackers
¼ cup melted butter**

HOW TO: Preheat oven to 375° F. Beat the egg yolks lightly. Add the condensed milk, lemon juice, and rind. Beat the egg whites with cream of tartar and salt until they hold stiff peaks. Gently fold into the yolk-milk-lemon mixture and blend well. Crush the graham crackers and add the melted butter. Line bottom only of an oblong ovenproof dish (8"x 12"). Pour in the lemon mixture and bake for 20 minutes. Let cool before serving. This keeps nicely in the refrigerator as well. Cut into squares.

FIBONACCI FLUFF

A refreshing, cool dessert, it puts out the fire after a spicy dinner, whether Italian, Indian, or Oriental. I named it for my publishing firm, partly because the name has such a euphonious sound, partly because the boss is partial to this dish.

This is a two-layered affair that must be made in two stages —a fluffy tapioca pudding goes on the bottom (first recipe), orange-flavored tapioca on top (second recipe). Bring it to the table in a glass serving bowl or glass dessert dishes—to get the full effect of the pudding variation in color and texture. May be made a day or two ahead of time. Serves 6.

Bottom layer
  3 tablespoons tapioca (Minute brand)
  3 tablespoons sugar
  1 egg yolk

⅛ teaspoon salt
  2 cups milk
  1 egg white
  2 tablespoons sugar
  ¾ teaspoon vanilla extract

HOW TO: Mix the tapioca, 3 tablespoons of sugar, egg yolk, salt, and milk in a saucepan. Let stand for 5 minutes. Beat the egg white until foamy. Gradually add 2 tablespoons of sugar to the egg white, beating to soft peaks —and set aside. Cook the tapioca mixture over medium heat until it reaches a full boil, stirring constantly, 6 to 8 minutes. Gradually add to the beaten egg white, stir quickly, until just blended. Stir in the vanilla extract. Cool for 20 minutes. Stir again. Pour into glass bowl and cool in the refrigerator to set.

Top layer
  ¼ cup tapioca (Minute brand)
  2½ cups orange juice

½ cup sugar
  Dash of salt

HOW TO: Put all the ingredients into a saucepan. Bring to a boil over medium heat, stirring often. Cool for 20 minutes. Stir well. To hasten the cooling process, pour from the cooking pan into a bowl. When cool, but not too firmly set, pour the orange juice and tapioca mixture over the cream tapioca pudding, and chill for at least 3 hours before serving.

RASPBERRY FOOLER

Here is a simple version of raspberry Bavarian pudding that is deliciously mouth-watering yet uncomplicated. It is a favorite of Ruth Simon, of Scarsdale, New York, active in cultural life in Westchester County. She finds it an elegant flourish following a fish or spicy meat dish. The double strength of the raspberry taste comes from using Danish Dessert, a handy Junket pudding, and frozen raspberries, both available year round. Yet for all its sweetness, it requires no sugar. Serves 6 to 8.

1 package (24) ladyfingers
2 tablespoons liqueur, Cointreau or Curaçao
2 packages Danish Dessert (a Junket product)
1¼ cups water

¾ cups raspberry juice from 1 package frozen raspberries
½ pint whipped heavy cream
2 tablespoons walnuts or pistachio nuts, crushed

HOW TO: Circle the interior of a 1½-quart soufflé dish with a vertical row of ladyfingers and cover the bottom with the remaining ladyfingers. Sprinkle lightly with liqueur. Thaw the raspberries and pour the juice into the water, to make a total of 2 cups of liquid. In a 1-quart saucepan put the Danish Dessert and liquid mixture, stirring constantly over low heat until the mixture comes to a boil, about 2 minutes. Allow it to boil for just 1 minute. Remove from heat. Transfer to a clean bowl and let cool in the refrigerator for about 1 hour. The mixture must not set. Fold in the raspberries. Whip ½ of the cream until stiff and fold into the cooled raspberry mixture. It will be a beautiful pink color. Pour the contents into the ladyfinger-lined soufflé dish. Refrigerate until set, about 2 hours. Before serving, whip the remaining cream to garnish the top, and sprinkle with the crushed nuts.

MAGIC APRICOT LEMON CAKE

Here's a bit of recipe round-robinry—a fabulous cake concoction that has traveled through several branches of the Day family and was then passed on to me by Beth Day, of Hanover, New Hampshire, in exchange for a few of my own. I am grateful to the whole family for the one cake I find goes with anything and everything whenever it's served.

Moist and delicate, it's a marvelous staple for cake lovers or a handsome specialty for birthday or anniversary occasions, or a cause for celebration all by itself. Can be made several weeks ahead and stored in the freezer. Underplayed with a thin coating of confectioners' sugar, lemon juice, and coconut shreds, or "dressed to kill" with whipped cream and strawberries, the basic preparation is still a cinch because Duncan Hines has gone to the trouble of mixing all the dry ingredients for you. (See photograph on page 78.) Serves 12.

1 package Duncan Hines Lemon
   Supreme Deluxe cake mix
¾ cup oil
1 can (12 ounces) apricot nectar
½ cup sugar
4 eggs, unbeaten

1 teaspoon lemon extract
Grated rind of 1 lemon
¾ cup confectioners' sugar
Juice of 1 lemon
1 teaspoon Cointreau or your
   favorite liqueur

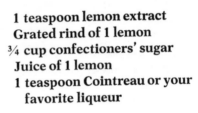

HOW TO: Preheat oven to 325° F. Grease and lightly dust with flour a bundt pan that has a center tube and is at least 4 to 5 inches deep. Place the first 7 ingredients in a large mixing bowl. Mix together thoroughly with an electric beater for 8 to 10 minutes. Do not cheat on the time required, it's your insurance for success. Pour into the bundt pan, allowing for a 2-inch rise in the dough, and bake for 1 hour (test with a toothpick). Cake will break slightly on top when done. After removal from the oven, let cool in the pan for about 5 minutes. Turn upside down onto a cake plate.

To make the icing, mix the confectioners' sugar, lemon juice, and a teaspoonful of your favorite liqueur, and drip over the top of the cake. This gives the cake its magic moistness. Trim with shredded coconut and sprinkle powdered sugar when completely cooled, if desired. For dressier occasions, serve with whipped cream and fresh berries.

10

Share The Loot

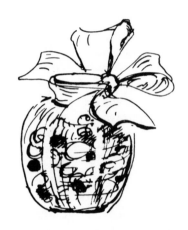

WARM THE HEART

Bring Pepper Jelly or Fromage Piquant
To warm the heart of a favorite Aunt.
Ham Casserole is portable and thrifty,
Elegant to serve, and the clean-up is nifty.

Tote a Tarragon Loaf for a picnic or sail.
Carry comfort with Custard to those who ail.
Try a Ruse with a Mousse for heavenly flavor.
Offer Burnt Almonds for your idol to savor.

RED HOT PEPPER JELLY

It took several long-distance phone calls to Florence Bloom in Laguna Hills, California, to verify every step in the creation of this piquant jelly. I'm glad to pass it on to my readers, toll free. This tangy touch of fire can be served as an hors d'oeuvre on crackers that have been spread with cream cheese, or used as a condiment to spark up a meat dish.

The ingredients are available year round, so you might want to mix up a batch before the holidays—any holidays—for gift-giving. In the meantime, make a habit of saving an assortment of small jars suitable for putting up jellies, so you'll be set when the spirit moves you. Yields 5 cups (40 ounces).

¼ cup crushed dried red pepper (Pepe rosso)
1 whole fresh red or green pepper, seeded and chopped fine
1¾ cups white vinegar

4 cups (2 pounds) sugar
1 bottle (6 ounces) Certo
¼ teaspoon red vegetable coloring
Paraffin for canning

HOW TO: Into a blender put the dried red pepper, fresh pepper, and ½ cup of the vinegar. Make a fine purée. It will yield ¾ of a cup. In a large saucepan put the sugar and the remainder of the vinegar. Slowly bring to a boil over low heat until the sugar is dissolved, about 15 minutes, stirring constantly. Add the pepper mixture and cook for 5 minutes more, stirring occasionally. Remove the saucepan from heat and stir in the Certo and the red food coloring, and mix well together. Pour into sterilized jars. Melt one bar of paraffin wax on the top of a double boiler over boiling water. Pour a little over each jar top to seal jelly.

FROMAGE PIQUANT

This homemade version of delectable Boursin cheese from France has all the nip and zip of the original. The recipe comes from Anne Denton Blair, a broadcast journalist of Washington, D.C., who offers this cheese to her guests as a preprandial treat in her charming Georgetown home. She made it at birthday party in my honor, and gifted me with the recipe as well. That's what I call a real friend.

Fromage Piquant may be kept up to two weeks in the re-frigerator and several months in the freezer. When ready to serve, let it thaw for about an hour. Offer it with melba toast rounds. Serves 6.

1 package (8 ounces) Borden's Lite-line Neufchatel cream cheese, at room temperature
1 tablespoon plain yogurt
2 cloves shallots, crushed
1 small clove garlic, crushed

½ teaspoon salt
1 teaspoon grated lemon rind
1 tablespoon chives or scallions, chopped fine
Freshly ground black pepper to taste

HOW TO: Mix the cheese and yogurt in a blender for a few seconds or mash with a fork until smooth. Add the shallots, chives or scallions, garlic, salt, and grated lemon rind. Mix the blend until smooth. Place in a small crock, with a few turns of freshly ground pepper on top. Chill in the refrigerator or freeze.

POTTED SHRIMP

Even for the hosts who have "everything"—and these couples are becoming more elusive as time goes by—there is always a homemade novelty to bring as a taste-teaser. This little spread goes with drinks and takes only a bit of your time to make. It's a soupçon of très radical chic to bring to friends to serve cold on toast or crackers. Yields enough for 4.

¼ pound (1 stick) butter
¼ pound very small fresh or frozen shrimp, shelled and deveined
⅛ teaspoon salt

Dash of cayenne pepper
⅛ teaspoon nutmeg
⅛ teaspoon allspice

HOW TO: Clarify the butter by heating it in a small saucepan over low heat until hot and foaming—be careful not to let it turn brown. Skim the foam off the top and then set aside 2 tablespoons of the clarified butter in a little container, to be used later. Transfer the remaining butter to a small skillet and add the shrimp, seasonings, and spices. Cook over moderate heat for 5 minutes, but do not allow butter to burn. Put the shrimp and sauce into a small container or glass jar. Pour the 2 tablespoons of clarified butter on top to seal the pot and put in the refrigerator to chill well.

141

CAVIAR PIE

A great way to serve caviar with all the trimmings in one dish. An elegant welcome gift to bring to a lucky hostess. Allow enough time to assemble all the ingredients. It requires no baking, just time to settle well in the refrigerator. Bring along very thin slices of black bread or unsalted crackers on which to serve the slices of this crustless pie. Serves 8.

Vegetable oil
5 hard-boiled eggs
½ pint sour cream at room
   temperature
1 jar (3½ ounces) black roe caviar
   (whitefish or lumpfish)

1 small onion, grated
1 tablespoon lemon juice
Paprika
Parsley flowerets
Black bread, sliced, or unsalted
   crackers

HOW TO: Oil a 9-inch glass pie plate on the bottom and sides. Put the hard-boiled eggs through a sieve or mash thoroughly with a fork. Press the mashed eggs into the bottom and sides of the pie plate to form a base for the caviar pie. Cover the eggs with a piece of wax paper and then set a smaller pie plate on top, pressing down to firm the egg "crust." Remove the top pie plate and refrigerate the wax-paper-topped, egg-lined dish.

About 2 or 3 hours before serving, open a jar of black roe caviar and turn it into a fine strainer to get rid of the juice. Remove the pie from the refrigerator and lift off the wax paper. Spread the caviar over the egg base. Then spread a layer of the onion over the caviar. Sprinkle with lemon juice. Spoon the softened sour cream over all, like an icing, being careful not to disturb the onion and caviar layers below.

To decorate, arrange a wreath of parsley flowerets around the edge of the pie. Place in the refrigerator to chill. When ready to transport, cover with aluminum foil and place in a flat box for convenient carrying.

MARINADE FOR BARBECUED LAMB

The wonderful flavor of this marinade comes from sherry. It's a culinary inspiration that belongs to Nancy Silbert of New York City, an interior designer who knows how to dazzle the palate as well as the eye.

Try it once at home and I think you will want to share it with friends. The second time around, double the quantities and put half of it up in a jar or bottle, to give with pride. Pass along with it these words of instruction: The meat and marinade should marry for 12 hours, with frequent turnings. The quantities below make 1 cup, enough for a barbecued lamb; double for gifting.

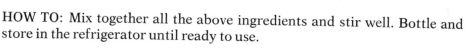

2 cloves garlic, minced
1 onion, finely chopped
3 tablespoons vegetable oil
1 cup medium dry sherry

Freshly ground black pepper
1½ teaspoons salt
½ teaspoon oregano
½ teaspoon thyme

HOW TO: Mix together all the above ingredients and stir well. Bottle and store in the refrigerator until ready to use.

A TIDY LEG OF LAMB

My occasional visits with Tessie Buchdahl, a professional masseuse, are a gaining proposition in many ways. As she pounds away, she plies me with easy and tasty recipes—working up a fine appetite that must be satisfied as soon as I get back to my kitchen. Is there a method to her massage?

She once shared with me this neat way to cook flavorful lamb. Next time you are asked to bring something to a big co-operative all-day feast, try it. Wrap the roast in aluminum foil for roasting and traveling. Serves 6 to 8.

1 leg of lamb
Salt and pepper to taste
1 tablespoon powdered ginger

2 cloves of garlic, crushed,
   or 1 tablespoon of garlic powder
1 glass orange juice

HOW TO: Trim as much skin and fat as possible from the leg of lamb. Season it with the salt, pepper, ginger, and garlic. Wrap the meat in aluminum foil and refrigerate overnight. When ready to roast, preheat oven to 300° F. Rest the covered leg of lamb in a shallow pan. Open the foil wrapping and bathe the lamb with a glass of orange juice. Recover with foil. Roast 30 to 35 minutes per pound. About ¾ of an hour before the meat is done, open the foil, increase the oven temperature to 400° F., and continue to roast until brown.

SUGGESTED WINE: MÉDOC (CLASSIC RED BORDEAUX) OR CABERNET SAUVIGNON (CALIFORNIA)

TARRAGON LOAF TO GO

When the hostess asks you for a communal picnic contribution, you will be ready-to-go with a Tarragon Loaf—chopped chicken and slivered ham in a rich jellied chicken broth flavored with tarragon. Prepare this a day ahead to free yourself for a care-free outing.

Gwen Reiman of Scarborough, New York, an architect who specializes in herb-garden design, says this is her family's all-time favorite. Serves 8.

4 pounds stewing chicken, cut into pieces
1 large onion, stuck with 2 cloves
1 bay leaf
2 carrots, quartered
2 parsley sprigs
2 tablespoons fresh tarragon, chopped, or 1½ teaspoons dried

2½ cups chicken broth (bouillon cubes will do)
1 envelope unflavored gelatin
¼ cup water
½ pound cooked ham, slivered
1½ cups celery, coarsely chopped (including leaves)
3 tablespoons parsley, chopped
2 tablespoons chives, chopped

HOW TO: In a heavy casserole place the chicken, onion, bay leaf, carrots, parsley, 1 tablespoon of fresh tarragon (or ¾ teaspoon of dried), and enough chicken broth to cover chicken half way up. Season with salt and pepper. Simmer, uncovered, for 30 minutes. Turn the chicken and simmer for another 30 minutes, or until tender. Cool in the broth. Remove the chicken pieces from the broth. Remove the skin and pick meat off the bones. Return the bones and skin to the broth. Simmer, uncovered, for 30 minutes. Strain broth and refrigerate. When cold, remove the congealed fat from the top.

Soften the gelatin in ¼ cup cold water. Reheat the broth to boiling and stir in the gelatin. Coarsely chop the chicken and season with salt and pepper. Rinse out a loaf pan (9″ x 5″ x 3″) with cold water. Arrange the slivered ham on the bottom. Mix together the chopped celery, parsley, chives, and remaining tarragon, and spread over the ham. Add the chicken and the broth. Press down the chicken so the broth barely rises to the surface. Chill overnight in the refrigerator.

When you arrive at your destination, unmold the loaf and surround with watercress. Cut into slices and serve with a lemon mayonnaise (see recipe on page 19).

SUGGESTED WINE: SAUVIGNON BLANC (CALIFORNIA, CHILLED)

DONALD'S CASSEROLE RECHERCHÉ

This tasty pie-crusted casserole really takes you off the beaten track. It's the kind of a mixture that true epicures will enjoy receiving. Donald Bruce White, the imaginative and talented caterer to whom busy socialites in the New York area turn for expert advice when planning their own dinner parties or running charitable affairs, contributed this idea toward elegant economy. Easy to assemble, and baked in a 1½-quart casserole, it can be brought to a supper party with pride. Serves 4.

1 ham steak, ½-inch thick
2 veal kidneys
1 medium-sized onion, coarsely chopped
½ pound mushrooms, cut into ½-inch-thick slices
¼ cup Madeira wine
2 tablespoons flour
2 cups chicken broth or veal stock, unsalted
1 9-inch pie crust, homemade or ready-frozen

HOW TO: Preheat oven to 350° F. Remove all the fat from the ham steak and the veal kidneys. Place the fat pieces in a heavy iron pot and heat quickly. Dice the ham steak into cubes, about ½-inch size. Remove the membranes from the kidneys and slice ¼-inch thick. Sauté the meats quickly in the fat and remove with a slotted spoon and set aside.

Sauté the onion in the fat until wilted, remove and then lightly sauté the mushrooms and remove also. Pour off the excess fat in the pan and remove any small fat particles. Deglaze the remaining fat by adding Madeira. Sprinkle in the flour to thicken the sauce and add the chicken broth or veal stock. Cook slowly until the sauce coats a spoon. Place the ham, kidney, onions, mushrooms and sauce into a casserole. Season only with a bit of pepper—the ham is salty enough. Place the crust on top of the casserole, sealing the edges. Bake until the crust is brown, about 45 to 50 minutes.

COMFORTING CUSTARD

Occasionally I look for something special to bring to a convalescing friend. Here's a treat suitable for youngsters as well as older people. It's a dish that makes anyone feel better right away. It can be kept in the refrigerator for several days' enjoyment. Thanks go to Doris Grunebaum of Scarsdale, New York, an accomplished hostess and thoughtful friend. Yields 6 individual custards.

3 cups warm milk
4 eggs
2 tablespoons sugar

Pinch of salt
1 teaspoon of vanilla extract
  or a pinch of nutmeg

HOW TO: Preheat oven to 300° F. Mix together all the ingredients. Pour into lightly greased individual custard cups and place the cups in a square pan (8"x 8"),with enough hot water in it to come ¾ inches high. Bake for about 1 hour. Test with a toothpick for firmness. Remove the pan from the oven and take out the custard cups and cool at room temperature or chill in the refrigerator. Place in a flat basket or covered carton to carry easily.

A RUSE WITH A MOUSSE

Whatever your hostess is serving as the main attraction for a sit-down dinner or a buffet, think about this superb finale if you have offered to bring dessert. Call it what you will—chocolate mousse, pôts de crème—it is the richest sweet-tooth satisfier at the end of a meal that I can offer. It comes originally from Angelica Klebanoff of Hewlett Harbor, Long Island, a fine cook with a round-the-world repertoire.

You may prepare this mousse a day in advance, in a large bowl or in individual sherbet dishes (the small plastic cocktail-sized glasses are convenient). Serves 8.

8 squares (½ ounce each) dark
  sweetened chocolate
6 tablespoons strong, liquid coffee
1½ tablespoons rum
5 eggs separated

½ teaspoon cream of tartar
Pinch of salt
½ pint heavy cream
2 tablespoons sugar
1 teaspoon vanilla extract

HOW TO: Break the chocolate into rough pieces and put in a saucepan with the coffee, and cook over low heat until completely melted. Beat the egg yolks well. Remove from heat and mix in the rum and add the beaten egg yolks. Beat the egg whites with cream of tartar and salt until they hold a stiff peak. Then carefully fold the whites into the chocolate-egg yolk mixture. Pour the mousse into 8 small sherbet dishes, soufflé dishes, or one large bowl, as you prefer. Chill at least 4 hours before serving. Top with the whipped cream that has been beaten with the sugar and vanilla extract.

GROUND NUT TORTE

Bringing a cake from your house to someone else's can sometimes be disastrous—especially when driving a car, one fast turn at a corner and the whole thing is liable to slide into disarray. Here is a glorious exception, guaranteed to take top honors at a cake sale, a bazaar, or wherever.

Among its many other virtues are advance preparation— it's better made a day or two ahead of time; it requires no flour, butter or salt, making it a fine gift for people on special diets. Serves 10.

6 eggs, separated
1 cup very fine granulated sugar
   (Superfine)
½ pound ground nuts, walnuts
   and pecans mixed, almonds, or
   filberts
1 teaspoon vanilla extract

1 teaspoon cream of tartar
1 cup heavy cream, whipped
1 small can (3 ounces) Hershey
   chocolate syrup
1 teaspoon strong, liquid coffee
1 or 2 teaspoons cognac
Bitter chocolate (optional)

HOW TO: Preheat oven to 325° F. Beat together the egg yolks and the sugar until thick, about 3 minutes. Fold in the ground nuts. (A blender is excellent for grinding the nuts.) Mixture will be very stiff. Add the vanilla extract. Beat the egg whites with cream of tartar until stiff. At first, fold a small amount of egg whites into the nut mixture until it becomes moist, and then fold in the remainder of the whites very carefully. Be sure to use a wooden spoon for this. Pour the batter into a well-greased 9-inch spring-form pan with tube center. (A center tube is important because the cake then bakes evenly, otherwise, it will fall in the middle.) Bake 1 hour. Test with tooth-pick for doneness. Some ovens require a little more time. When cool, invert cake and remove spring-form.

When ready to serve, make a topping of whipped cream and chocolate syrup mixed with the coffee and cognac. This gives it a wonderful mocha flavor. Cover all sides of the nut torte. If desired, shave bitter chocolate over the top for a fancy fillip. Refrigerate up to 1 hour before serving.

BURNT ALMONDS

Not to be confused with a burnt offering, this delicacy is a year-round gift possibility. The quantities may be doubled, tripled, or quadrupled — depending upon your needs. Make these Burnt Almonds in small batches, to be sure to control the results. The nuts keep indefinitely in a glass jar. If you have artsy-craftsy tendencies, you might want to add your own label to dress up your gift.

½ **pound unblanched almonds**
½ **cup sugar**
½ **cup water**

HOW TO: Boil all the above ingredients together in a saucepan, stirring constantly over medium heat until the sugar and syrup have disappeared. You will be left with nice, powdery coated almonds. Now continue heating and stirring until the powder once again begins to take a liquid form. It will carmelize and glaze the nuts. Remove the nuts from the pan onto a cookie sheet, and separate each from its neighbors before they cool. The entire cooking process takes ½ hour—not a minute more or less, so don't get discouraged while stirring the powdered form, it will eventually car-melize. Be patient, the result is worth it.

148

HEDDA HENDRIX believes fashions in food have changed just as radically as other life styles. She introduces a new kind of cook-think to the culinary scene. Her message is simple: With a zestful approach, one can make home-cooking a delightful experience and a satisfying hobby instead of a humdrum chore. In her former professional career in public relations, the author organized a variety of special events for such diverse interests as Lane Bryant, Inc.; the Orchestral Society of Westchester; and Channel 13, the NYC educational TV station: planning the arrangements, decor and menus for large social or fund-raising functions. She has written articles for numerous publications.

Ms. Hendrix has also been an active volunteer in civic affairs. She was honored for her accomplishments by the NYC Chapter, American Institute of Architects, and Channel 13.

Married to an architect, she and her husband make their home in New York City and Northern Westchester County, N.Y., where they tend a well-loved house and garden.

RICHARD COE, the illustrator, is a landscape painter who teaches water-color painting of wild flowers at the Kitchawan Station of the Brooklyn Botanic Gardens. He and his wife live in Goldens Bridge, N.Y., where they pursue herb culture as an avocation.

RONNIE KAUFMAN, the photographer, has studied at the School of Visual Arts and with Philippe Halsman in New York. Her work has appeared in shows, magazines and educational film strips. A native Californian, she lives in Santa Monica with her husband and children.

149

INDEX